V. S. NAIPAUL

TRANSFORMING SUBALTERN CONSCIOUSNESS: A CRITICAL ANALYSIS OF V. S. NAIPAUL'S WORKS

GHANSHYAM PAL

Dedicated to my parents whose love, support, and encouragement are integral part of this book

Contents

Acknowledgements

I take this opportunity to express my gratitude to all those writers and critics whose literary collections have offered me food for thought.

My deep sense of gratitude goes to my esteemed teacher Prof. Surekha Dangwal, Vice-Chancellor, Doon University, Dehradun, for her help, advice, support and guidance. Her recommendations and suggestions have been invaluable for the successful completion of this book. Special thanks to my parents, particularly my father, for giving me liberty and strength I needed to complete my work. Words alone cannot express the thanks that I owe to them for their love and support. Sincere thanks are also due to their family members and my colleagues and friends who endured this long process with me, always offering me encouragement and support.

Last but not the least, I would like to thank Notion Publisher & Distributers (P) Ltd. For publishing the book in a very nice shape.

Preface

I started reading works by V. S. Naipaul during the 2013th when I was doing research in HNB Garhwal Central university in Uttarakhand and Naipaul was one of those writers from former colonies offering new perspectives on the world. His fiction undergoes certain paradigmatic shifts especially in the presentation of the representative subaltern and diasporic ambivalence among certain protagonists and other characters. His fiction is a parallel journey signifying his personal growth and ultimate mature perception. His treatment of the theme of "subaltern" under postcolonial umbrella is penetrating and comprehensive as he shares the anguish of colonial expatriates throughout his career. His novels are not merely reflections of abstraction; rather, they are packed with thought. I began to write research papers on his novels such as *Nostalgia through Diasporic perspective in A House for Mr. Biswas, A Journey towards Self Discovery in V. S. Naipaul's Magic Seeds*, and *Cultural Crisis in V.S. Naipaul's A House for Mr. Biswas.*

This book entitled ***Transforming Subaltern Consciousness: A Critical Analysis of V.S. Naipaul Works*** presents critical analysis and assessment of Naipaul's fictions, attempts to restate the fact that Naipaul is the most prominent postcolonial expatriate novelists having first hand colonial experience. His novels deal with the colonial as well as postcolonial societies with an explicit account of common complexities inherent among the marginalized societies.

On the whole, Naipaul in his fiction puts continuous emphasis on the voices of subaltern, diasporic and marginalized people within postcolonial context. His oeuvre commonly speaks of expatriation, exile and the people who have been side-lined and discriminated from the society due to caste, class, gender and ethnicity.

The book is divided into six chapters including conclusion. The first chapter i.e., Introduction deals with the critical survey of postcolonial literature and its many aspects like subaltern and diaspora in terms of caste, class, gender and location. The introduction chapter of the book provides a detailed understanding of the impact of subaltern and diaspora literature under postcolonial umbrella. Critics like Gayatri Chakravarty Spivak, Antonio Gramsci and Ranajit Guha have been discussed with their texts at length to expound the subaltern discourse. No doubt postcolonial is a big sea and one becomes '*other*' in one's country and here begins the process of 'otherization'. One feels '*other*' because of caste, class and gender. One has to face discrimination in society on the basis of outsider, caste, ethnicity and gender. The book also throws light on the scenario in which a person becomes subaltern in a diaspora location.

The second chapter entitled "Gendered Subalternism and Myth of Masculinity" deals with imbalance discourse in the proceeding novels such as *A House for Mr. Biswas, Half a Life and Magic Seeds*. In this chapter Naipaul made an attempt to explore major female characters like Shamas, Sarojini and Dehuti and their psychological states of mind seasoned with patriarchy. A strong gender bias has been felt in Naipaul's treatment and projection of female characters widely displays two broader categories of female characters— dominating and their subordinates. Regardless of their position in society they have a very little to say in their husband's lives.

Naipaul draws the distinction as a major setback for the progress of Indians in an alien and heterogeneous society. A feminist analysis brings out the untouched aspect of gender present in Naipaul's novels. In Indian society the female characters in Naipaul's novels are secondary, unsympathetic character and remain on margin. Thus, they have suffered doubly unlike women of the white world. They have suffered first on account of their race and class and then gender.

"Politics of Ethnicity and Subaltern Voices" is third chapter and Naipaul's Indian trilogy has been analysed with unravelling observations on India. It highlights the soaring wounds which shattered his image of India. It brings Naipaul's attitude towards India and justifies his natural contempt for Indian culture and its people. The book reveals the instances where Naipaul's myth regarding India has been shattered. It is an answer to Naipaul's bitter and pungent reaction to Indian life style. In his famous Indian trilogy— *An Area of Darkness, Indian: A Wounded Civilization* and *India: A Million Mutinies Now,* Naipaul meticulously scrutinizes and demythologizes Indian culture. His myths of India as a golden land, as a dream destination, as a proud lineage were all demolished in one blow of reality hitting on the front. It made him almost hysterical, which he took years to come out of. Consequently, his writings on India bear negative trait.

The book reveals Naipaul's narrow view and mean remarks about Indian culture without considering the real significance. George Lamming states that his "Eurocentric attitude" is responsible for his scorn. He is thus bound to evaluate "orient" from a European parameter. It leads to disappointment and distress for an "insider-outsider" person like Naipaul.

Naipaul's using derogatory words for India and her culture shows his trick to present the nation as a land of primitives and serpent charmer before the eyes of western for the sake of getting name and fame. While using Indian myth Naipaul hardly bothers about the importance of those myths. He has done this intentionally as a politics to lower India's image and win laurels for himself.

The fourth chapter "*In a Free State* and *A Bend in the River:* The Psychology of Marginalization in Diasporic Location" deals with diasporic concerns and a psychology of marginalization in diasporic location. In these novels, one can see the postcolonial disorder, inter-tribal conflicts and the problems of identity because the characters of these novels are diasporic and marginalized. Both these novels offer "sombre accounts of chaos at the time of the African transition to post colonialism, foregrounding the lack of a coherent ideology or leadership that might fill the vacuum left by the old political order" (Hawley 307-8). Both the novels depict Naipaul's vision of a free and fair world whose inhabitants might rise above the barriers of nation or nationality, and might consider themselves as the citizens of the world.

The paradoxes and ambiguities are significant factors in Naipaul's works. The paradoxes reflect the complexity of Naipaul as a former colonial subject whose origins were multi-cultural, and who acquired a multiple self. Naipaul's subaltern depiction is unique in its complexity and significant in today's multicultural society.

Chapter five is "Caste, Ethnicity and Social Fragmentation in *The Suffrage of Elvira* and *The Mimic Men*." This chapter is a modest attempt to view some of the problems faced by the diasporic community due to their caste and ethnicity in the settled society. Almost all the diasporic communities face initial problems and sufferings when they settle in a new land. Among the problems that diasporic communities face in the settled country are discrimination and social fragmentation. Discrimination is the leading trauma, which upsets them most. The plants when plucked from a soil and planted in a new one has survival problem; similarly, the diasporic community too faces problem of survival. They have to adjust to the environment, language, culture and the society.

The writer presents dispossessed people who search for order in their lives. His postmodern and postcolonial status leads him to focus mainly on the problem of contemporary world struggling with the question with identity and Naipaul deviates from this question. In his wide range of writing, he covers up almost all the continents of the world as his travel is worldwide. He expresses candidly what he felt during those travels which aroused fervour all over the world.

The conclusion brings into sharp focus the diverse patterns of ambivalence underlying existential search of a portion for the earth that runs beneath Naipaul's fictional works from the beginning to end. An analysis is made as how the past, in Naipaul's fiction, asserts itself through appreciation of tradition and how the former colonial subjects, dispossessed of their native tradition, are obsessed with regaining a distinctive identity. His travels along with his personal experience of rootlessness, made him emphatic in presenting the alienating effects of colonial past on today's postcolonial people

The book ends with a comprehensive bibliographic list that will enable the scholars of English Literature to pursue their study further. The book is ideal for all students, research scholars and teachers of English Literature because Naipaul opened a new vista for Postcolonial Literature.

Ghanshyam Pal

Introduction

V. S. Naipaul (1932-) is considered to be one of the most prominent postcolonial expatriate novelists having first hand colonial experience. His novels deal with the colonial as well as postcolonial societies with an explicit account of common complexities inherent among the marginalized societies. Naipaul's work is commonly regarded as an implicit biography of his departure from the narrow background of the Caribbean Island to the open cosmopolitan culture of the world at large. He carries three conflicting, and at times, interacting component in his personality of "being a Trinidadian colonial, an English metropolitan, and a person of Indian ancestry" (Sanjiv Kumar iv).

This Trinidadian born writer never acknowledges his association with his mother land. Mentioning Trinidad Naipaul accepts that he has minimum contact with members of other races and that he has met people who were outside of his ethnic group only in official contexts where it has been extremely necessary. Many times, he has described his stay in Trinidad as a complete waste of time. The unpromising land of Trinidad was stifling to his spirit. Trinidadian Hindu family life in its miniature form seemed irrelevant and meaningless. Although Naipaul never relished his Trinidadian roots, he always felt a warm approximation with the members of his family particularly his father whose metaphysical anguish he could easily comprehend and appreciate.

The father of Naipaul was his guide, mentor and a constant source of literary inspiration. He aroused in his son the passion and ambition to become a writer and gave him the idea of stories that could be written about colonial and marginalized life in Trinidad. He himself acknowledges his father's contribution when he says that the ambition to be writer was given to him by his father. Naipaul had immense protective care and affection for his father because his father was a failed writer. Father failure spurred in him a writing spirit. In one way it was the direct encouragement of his father that helped young Naipaul to set his eyes on writing career in his formative years.

When Naipaul went to London on scholarship for higher education at the age of eighteen, he had a chance to escape route from the constraining limitations of a corroded colonial life. On reaching London, he felt that it was the center from where he could launch his literary career. Not only the father's profligacy but his own constant anxiety of living in unstable homes, and ultimately the consciousness of "half-made societies" provided the backdrop to Naipaul's neurosis. Since "neurosis" is seen as a flood gate of creative overture, Naipaul, in his writing career spanning almost fifty years now, has produced a staggering amount of literature ranging from fiction, non-fiction, travelogue and autobiographical essays.

Naipaul's life has been rootless and adrift in many ways. The young Naipaul lived within an Indian community cut off from Trinidad's Creole society. In other words, Naipaul lacked connections both to his Indian roots and to Trinidad's Creole society. In addition, the administrative center of colonial government, or London, was far away and had an image of inaccessibility. His sense of up-rootedness was intensified by the fact that his family moved from house to house. His leaving for England increased his sense of rootlessness as well. When he first came to England, he had a great sense of being adrift.

Such background information brings forth one of the ubiquitous themes of rootlessness in his work. Many of his characters are adrift. They are away from their own society or lack such a community from birth. For individuals, the disconnection from societies is both the source of their freedom and the cause of their distress. Many of the characters choose to be away from their own society for their own benefit. Even the characters under a forced exile see the advantages to their free situation. However, Naipaul also shows that there is a price to pay in exchange for gaining personal freedom. Achieving personal freedom is depicted as causing a feeling of isolation, reducing any sense of responsibility, or lessening a genuine human connection.

Naipaul regards himself as a former colonial who has become a homeless cosmopolitan. Owing to his ability to write more about himself and his past, he can be seen as someone who has projected much of his personal experiences of the contemporary world into literature. His unique experience is representative of the major social, psychological, political and cultural change of our time. The novel taken up for study represents East-Indian Trinidadian communities into which he was born and brought up. The historical experiences of the multicultural Trinidadian community employed almost exclusively in agricultural labor under indenture system. They carry with them mainly rural experiences of British India, their inherent differences and their native cultural contexts through the migratory process. Their fondness of home culture and its associated implications are integral parts of their being.

With the passage of time, the emigrant communities that settled as labor class multiplied, and by the mid-twentieth century these expatriates claimed the major portion of the population of Trinidad. Nasser Mustapha has given a data-based account of the Indian immigrants when he observes:

The majority of Indian immigrants coming to the Caribbean were from the United Provinces (UP) and Bihar. The Indians who came to the Caribbean tried to recapture their religion as they knew it back in India, and to establish it under the new and challenging circumstances. They viewed the wider Creole society with suspicion. Being separated from their families back in India, religion served as a bond with their homeland during their supposedly temporary sojourn in this strange land. Religion gave their lives direction and a sense of completeness. (133-134)

As the time passes, the concept of acculturation affected the overseas communities in due course, and East-Indian communities of Trinidad underwent a sort of osmosis. In their deliberate effort to preserve their customs, rites, traditions, religion, languages, caste beliefs and their family patterns, they got themselves transformed so as to familiarize themselves to the colonial setting of creolized society of Trinidad. It was impossible for the East-Indian expatiate in Trinidad to maintain their homogenous cultural identity.

In his early fictions V. S. Naipaul captures twice-torn and displaced immigrants oscillating between home culture and alien culture on the one hand and obviously fascinated by the sophisticated culture of the Westerners on the other hand. The novels expose the essential ambivalence of East-Indian emigrants at Trinidad seeking belongingness and affiliation there in the West. To present the apparent cultural confusion has been the obsession of diasporic writing, but Naipaul's account of these dispossessed is based on his first-hand experiences and thus seems quite authentic. Jasbir Jain elucidates:

There is need to realize the significance of the cultural encounter which takes place in diasporic writing, the bicultural pulls and creation of a new culture which finally emerges . . .. Diasporic writing has developed a double vision. The expatriate as he moves from one culture to another may need to locate in relation to the centre. (15-16)

Naipaul's writing is caught up in a tension between a quest for personal freedom and a counter quest for a sense of belonging. Naipaul, as a rootless man, idealizes society in which people are settled, share values, and have an organic relation with the place. Yet he also knows the joy of rootlessness, so he is skeptical about whether anyone will appreciate the individual's complete belonging to the land. Thus, Naipaul simultaneously and paradoxically longs for individual freedom and a sense of belonging.

Naipaul has multiple origins to which he only partially relates. This makes Naipaul's achieving a sense of belonging difficult. The nature of colonial education encouraged Naipaul in his identification with the values of English civilization. On the other hand, he is consciously aware of his ethnic roots as an Indian, and reveals a Hindu morality in his works. His self-recognition as a colonial subject is also strong. His colonial identification defines the destinations of his journeys. For instance, through the journeys of postcolonial nations, Naipaul reflects not only on postcolonial conditions, but also on his own circumstances. However, Naipaul belongs to none of these origins completely. Consequently, his search for his roots is caught in an unfruitful repetition.

These multiple heritages also cause inconsistency and ambiguity in Naipaul. For instance, he reveals an unresolved ambivalence in his attitude towards the history of empire. He sees colonial rule both as a system of vile plunder and as a lost ideal of order; he views the metropolitan centre both as fulfilling and betraying.

These aspects of rootlessness, multiple heritages and ambiguous belongingness are the significance themes of the author. Naipaul is deprived of a consistent identity, a sense of security, and a sense of belonging to a certain culture as a consequence of cultural transplantation caused by imperialism. Naipaul embodies the aftermath of imperialism and the condition of the postcolonial era.

Naipaul is determined to write truthfully to himself. Although the spontaneous and honest responses sometimes reveal inconsistencies or cause disputes against him, the value of his writing is its frankness and confidence. Naipaul's critical perception ranges from harsh condemnation to the highest critical praise. Much of the controversy over his works stems from the way in which his incisive and honest vision is perceived. Since Naipaul's methods of searching for truth depends on autobiographical themes, the overemphasis on the ideological issue seems inappropriate. This thesis, therefore, will try to balance autobiographical accounts with the political aspects of Naipaul's writings.

Indeed, ever since the publication of his first book *The Mystic Masseur*in 1957, he has been seen as a prominent diaspora writer. Very much like the characters in the book, his life reflects queer sense of displacement and restlessness. It is this restlessness of the novelist that helps him to portray the postcolonial diaspora anguish with intensity and authority. A Trinidadian by birth and Indian by descent from a family of Indian indentures laborers; and a Londoner for his English education and his stay in England, Naipaul cannot call any place his home or cannot take any place for granted. Wherever he went he could, at best, remain a visitor. Rootlessness was something that never ceased to haunt Naipaul and he never stopped reminding himself about his Hindu origins and beliefs of his Indian ancestors settled in the Caribbean.

Naipaul's works of fictions comprise - *The Mystic Masseur* (1957, *The Suffrage of Elvira* (1958), *Miguel Street* (1959, *A House for Mr. Biswas* (1961), *Mr. Stone and the Knights Companion* (1963), *The Mimic Man* and *A Flag on the Island* (1967), In *a Free Street* (1971), *A Bend in the River* (1979), *The Enigma of Arrival* (1987), *Half a Life* (2001) and *Magic Seeds* (2004).

In 1960 he began to travel. *The Middle Passage* (1962) records his impressions of colonial society in the West Indian and South America. *An Area of Darkness* (1964), *India: A Wounded Civilization* (1977) and *India: A Million Mutinies Now* (1990) form his acclaimed 'Indian Trilogy'. *Letters Between a father and Son,* the early correspondence between the author and his family, appeared in 1990, followed by two essay collection, *The Writer and the World* and *A Writer's People* in 2002 and 2007.

As a result of his enormous literary product, he has received many distinguished awards. He received **John Llewelyn Rhyn Memorial Prize** for *The Mystic Masseur,*his first novel in 1957. His next two novels brought him **Somerest MaughamAward**. He bagged the prestigious **HawthorndenPrize** for *Mr. Stone and the Knights Companion* and **W. H. SmithAward** for the next novel, *The Mimic Men*in 1967. For his novel *In a Free State*in 1971, he received **Booker Prize**. As a reputed writer he has received the **Knighthood** in 1990. He won the first **DavidCohen British Literature Prize** for life – time achievement in 1993. He got the most prestigious **Nobel Prize** in 2001for literature. No doubt, he is the most admired contemporary novelist for his dissecting tone and piquant style of narration today.

The genesis of diaspora, penetration of the writer's consciousness and the reluctant expatriate sensibility that gave birth to cross cultural writing is the context in which Naipaul's love-hate relationship with India and Trinidad is highlighted in his oeuvre. Naipaul has also recorded that he had been brought up in a double world; the closed Hindu world of his grandmother's family and the outside world. Both these worlds were incompatible. That is why most of the works of Naipaul are the outcome of his personal enigma of being a displaced member of a minority race and religion in Trinidad. As it is quite clear in the works of Naipaul that racial and compartmentalization of the Caribbean caused by slavery and colonization, led the earlier West Indian writers to write basically about their communities, who treated the outsiders only as caricatures or figures of fun.

The multiple heritage of Naipaul puts him into a position that makes it possible for him to present an objective account of his subjective experience. Naipaul became a man of broader outlook. He seems to negate both Trinidad and India as his possible homes. He has been criticized many times for being the representative of imperialism. His works condemn this castigating view straightforwardly as he hardly ever shows his inclination or belongingness to England except for momentary comfort after experiencing the torturing expatriate feeling of being un-housed, displaced and alienated in Trinidad.

Naipaul has experienced different cultures to reach to the conclusion that the fragmentation and alienation happen to be the universal predicament of a man in the present-day world. At the same time, he happens to be concerned with the portrayal of the predicament of man living in a postcolonial society. The very same leads him to be a representative of the predicament of the universal modern man. Naipaul rises from the position of a man who experiences and articulates the concerns of universal humanity. The most important influences responsible for making him a typical diasporic writer was Trinidad, his birthplace consisting of diverse races, culture, religions and psyches. The society of Trinidad was devoid of any sense of nationality or recognition as the people were in a perpetual dilemma regarding the uncertainty about their affiliations. They were in confusion whether to feel proud of their original identities or to get themselves readily assimilated with the Trinidadian culture.

Thus, subaltern consciousness has been a favorite theme of expatriate writers. Different postcolonial themes like the theme of identity crisis, fractured/torn-identities, East-West encounters, rejection, anxiety, love-hate relationship within two cultures, homelessness, migration, expatriation, displacement, uprooting from the homeland, belongingness, cultural adaption, political insurgency, the feeling of no-where-ness etc., reflecting subalternism and diasporic ambivalence are projected in the writings of V. S. Naipaul.

Subaltern: The Process of 'Otherization' in Terms of Caste, Class, Gender and Location

Every society has always remained categorized since time immemorial and subaltern issues are the outcome of these categorizations. In the society, basically there are three types of people – the first one is the mainstream, who have full power to fulfil their Wish in the society – the upper class, the second one is alternative, who have less power than the mainstream, but have much power than the other, who are called as the middle class and the third one is the voiceless or lower-class people, who are always dominated and neglected by those two classes of people. According to Concise Oxford Dictionary, these voiceless people termed as a 'subaltern' or the man of 'inferior rank'.

The etymological meaning of subaltern is below the rank. The British Military officer used this term for their junior subordinates. *The Concise Oxford English Dictionary* explains the term subaltern as, "an officer in the British army below the rank of captain, especially a second lieutenant" (Oxford 1434). Some thinkers use this term for marginalized groups and the lower classes. They explain subaltern is, "a person rendered without agency by his or her social status" (Young 67).

The concept of subaltern is related to history and society in terms of politics, economics and sociology of subalternity with attitudes, ideologies and belief systems. In a nut shell the culture represents the condition. The word 'Subaltern' came from Italian word '*Subaterno*.' On the other hand, in its literal meaning it is used in the defence where a lower graded army person, who has to obey his officer or boss and work in the subordination. The word cannot be understood except as one of the constitutive terms in a binary relationship of which the '*other*' is in domination.

But the meaning of subaltern is a much-debated concept among the postcolonial scholars. The history of subaltern is not clearly explained but Marxist philosopher and theorist Antonio Gramsci (1891-1937) influenced

Subaltern Studies Group, a group of South Asian historians and explored the role of non-elite actors in South Asian history. The thinkers of the group used the term firstly in a non-military sense. It is believed that Gramsci, "used the term as a synonym for proletariat, possibly as a code word in order to get his writings post prison censors, while others believe his usage to be more nuanced and less clear cut" (Morton 156).

Today, critical theorists are paying attention to the subalterns who are neglected in society in many ways under the subaltern Studies. Antonio Gramsci begins Subaltern Studies in England in 1970. He used the word 'Subaltern' first in his Prison Notebooks (1971). He writes a symbol of an intellectual communism of Italian manufacture, which referred to the class, gender, race, language and culture.

Gramsci's subaltern classes present the subordination of class, caste, and gender which are lower rank of human beings in the rigid classification of South Asian Sociology. Subaltern classes cover woman, dalit, black, children, peasants, workers, labourers and other groups who were denied access to "hegemonic power" (Ashcroft 215). Subaltern is a term which is used in postcolonial theory and since 1970's onwards the term is regularly used as a reference to colonized people in the South Asian subcontinent. And now, this term has become an area of study in history, anthropology, sociology and literature. Thus, Antonio Gramsci used subaltern for those groups of people who are victims of hegemony of the upper and ruling classes.

Gayatri Chakravarty Spivak explains subaltern's emotion in reality in her most famous essay, "Can the Subaltern Speak? (1985)" that the subaltern cannot speak until their conditions may not be historically improved. According to her, subaltern is not a classy word for the oppressed. She explains:

Everything that has limited or no access to the cultural imperialism is subaltern- a space of difference. Now who would say that's just the oppressed? The working class is oppressed. It's not subalterns. (De Kock 23)

In literature, subaltern is a non-western and postcolonial concept which is generally used for downtrodden belonging to the lower caste and class, weak sex and economically poor groups in the rigid social strata of the developing countries of Asia, Africa and Latin America, known as Third World Nations. The progressive historians started the Subaltern Studies as a project for revising Indian historiography on the basis of subaltern perspective. The main aim of this project was to collect strong and authentic historical evidences for covering maximum aspect of Indian history. They collected and compiled large number of colonial and post-colonial India's social, economic and religious issues based on peasants and insurgencies. On the support of the project Gayatri Chakravarty Spivak comments, "The most significant outcome of this revision or shift in perspective is that the agency of change is located in the insurgent or the subaltern" (Spivak 330).

Being a subaltern historian and feminist critique of postcolonial era, Gayatri Chakravarty Spivak made two necessary distinctions in the research work of subaltern studies about the peasant revolt and as well as inside the domain of colonial governance. The one is about the structural model of subaltern consciousness- a 'pure' structure and the other is about the shapes and forms for appearing a history. She also mentioned women as a subaltern of the contemporary society as she said at the end of her essay:

> Can the subaltern speak? As the subaltern cannot speak. There is no virtue in global laundry lists with 'women' as pious item. Representation has not withered away. Female intellectual has a circumscribed task which she must not disown with a flourish. (Spivak 279)

Subalternity is a kind of subordinate and exterior positionality in relation to a hegemonic power relation, a relation that is constituted by and operates through both structural power and the normalized forms of knowledge and subjectivity of those who participate in it. Subalterns, then, are both disempowered and expelled by the hegemonic relation because they do not speak within the terms of its form of problematization and its rules for legitimate consent and dissent. It is not that the subaltern cannot speak at all; they speak within the terms of the hegemonic relation, or in a way that is legible or recognizable to the hegemony. Thus, subalternity is a positionality or moment in relation to hegemony. In this way practices, subjectivities, knowledge and normativity can be subalternized, but each can also be subalternized in full or in part, depending on the constitution of the hegemonic relation itself, and in relation to multiple and crisscrossing hegemonies.

In subaltern study, the notion of the '*Other*'has always been an important topic examined by philosophers, historians and anthropologists. Throughout the history, the '*Other*'has been described as "the quintessence of another individual who was different from the inner self" (Sarukkai 58). But the recognition of the '*Other*' has also meant its contact/relationship with the self. In fact, the act of '*Othering*' is a manifestation of power relations. When we start describing ourselves as part of a group of people united in a 'we', while other people are constructed as fundamentally different, united in a 'they', we are using a powerful weapon that might serve to delegitimize others. And too often, these distinctions are drawn along the classic axis of discrimination and power differences, like sexuality, gender, ethnicity, race, class and so on.

According to Michel Foucault, '*Othering*' is strongly connected with "power and knowledge" and "power is a social construct" (Foucault 87). The society points out the perceived weaknesses of the weak section to make oneself look stronger or better. It implies a hierarchy, and it serves to keep power where it already lies. Colonialism is one such example of the powers of '*Othering*.' According to Stuart Hall, "Identity is not only important for its political aspect, but also for its foundation of culture and representation of the individual and the society" (Hall 234). The psychological aspect of culture is the bridge connected to the global identities of an individual and the most important "psychological aspect of culture - the bridge between culture and personality – is the identification process. This process is most certainly a major impediment to cross-cultural understanding" (Hall 240). In other words, by discovering and appreciating the '*other*', people can recognize culture as a tool for fostering mutual understanding, establishing relationships among countries and promoting social cohesion.

Practically, otherization has two levels- social and political. On the social level, otherization of any person by a group based upon class, race, ethnicity, gender or religion, is to differentiate the group from another so as to exclude the latter, whom one wants to subordinate or subjugate. On the political level, the otherization of non-Western culture by Western people meant to establish their superiority over the rest of the world. In conventional circumstances, the Western treat non-Western people as '*other*' in order to show them as different from and superior to latter.

In the Postcolonial fiction of V. S. Naipaul, terms like 'Other', 'Exile', 'Diaspora', and 'Dispossession', in reference to the caste and class have historical and cultural significance. The critical theories of Bhabha, Gayatri Spivak and Edward Said can be conveniently applied to explore the cultural and political tensions of the colonized people depicted in the works of Naipaul. Paul Gilroy in his historical defense of the multicultural society in *Postcolonial Melancholia* (2002) analyses the impact of race, politics and culture of the colonized people and their multilayered traumas of life.

Bhabha begins by contending that colonial discourse depends on the "concept of fixity in the ideological construction of otherness. This fixity is the sign of cultural/historical/racial difference" (Bhabha 18). Its major discursive strategy is the stereotype which Bhabha defines as a "form of knowledge and identification that vacillates between what is always in place, already known, and something that must be anxiously repeated" (Bhabha 18).

According to Bhabha colonial discourse produces the colonized as a fixed reality which is at once another and yet entirely knowable and visible. It resembles a form of narrative whereby the productivity and circulation of subjects and signs are bound in a reformed and recognizable totality. It employs a "system of representation, a regime of truth that is structurally similar to realism" (Bhabha 23).

Regarding national culture, Frantz Fanon focuses on the effects of the hegemonic devices used by the colonizers to obliterate the culture of the colonized and the resulting desire of the colonized to unite under a homogenous national identity and culture. He says, "Colonial domination, because it is total and tends to over-simplify, very soon manages to disrupt in spectacular fashion the cultural life of the conquered people" (Fanon 236). Colonialism is not only satisfied with emptying the native's brain of all form and content but it:

Distorts, disfigures and destroys the history of the colonized people. Therefore, colonial rulers propagated a false belief that colonialism came to lighten their darkness. The colonizers focused on convincing the colonized that if the settlers were to leave, the natives would at once fall back into barbarism, degradation and bestiality. (Fanon 180)

The concept of "subalternity" emanated from the academic field of postcolonial studies to describe a group of marginalized people. Giving priority to one group naturally creates the '*other*'. Pushing certain groups to the margin, to the periphery, away from the vitality and vivacity of the centre necessarily involves the process of cultural *othering*. Simone de Beauvoir elaborates the process of *cultural othering*:

She is defined and differentiated with reference to man and not he with reference to her; she is the incidental, the inessential as opposed to the essential. He is the Subject; he is the Absolute – she is the other. (16)

Thus, the subaltern is created and burdened with the subordinated dimensions always on the right side of the binary oppositions. It is, however, imperative to note that in postcolonial theory, the concept of subaltern is an overused term, randomly used to refer to anyone who is politically/ economically marginalized. Such academic co-options of the term have led Spivak to criticize academic opportunism that seeks to gain a privileged space in the name of subaltern representation. In her seminal essay on the issue "*Can the Subaltern Speak*?" Spivak claims that the historical and structural condition of political representation does not guarantee that the interests of the particular subaltern groups will be recognized or that their voice will be heard. She further mentions that the general difference between aesthetic and political structures of representation is that aesthetic representation tends to foreground its status as a re-presentation of the real, whereas political representation denies this structure of representation. "A subaltern is a person without lines of social mobility" (Morton 54).

The subaltern is imbued with the negatives at all levels, be it social, cultural, sexual or personal. The subaltern is the one who is denied an authentic presence. (S) he is the one bereft of voice or dignity: one who is a mere zero, a cipher with no essential meaning or a sense of being. The gravity of the situation is intensified when the subaltern is a woman. She is even denied a subject position. Being at the precarious juncture and crisscrossed by multiple forces of oppression, she is the one who occupies the lowest position in the social ladder. Her presence is not even authenticated; if at all it is done, it is only to enforce the superiority of the male counterpart. She is the deviant, the deform ant, signifying all the lacks and voids. The word subaltern can be defined as "the general attribute of subordination whether it is expressed in terms of class, caste, age, gender and office or in any other way" (Guha 3).

The predicament of the female subaltern is the most miserable of all oppressive states. It is a lethal combination for the subaltern to be a woman. Her life, dreams, hopes and the basic right to a dignified survival is thwarted by multiple forces of oppression. She is a victim of racism, classism, and most importantly, of the primarily subjugating ideology of patriarchy.

Literature predominantly controlled by masculine canons of aesthetics, projects womanhood as an ideal to be achieved. Those who do not adhere to the ideal are the deviants, the deferments and the incarnations of devil himself. She is a passive muted victim, the epitome of unquestioning obedience or the witch capable of engulfing everything in the fire of her lunacy. The real woman is lost somewhere in the process. Her hopes and wails are silenced forever. She continues to have a veiled existence, the veil signifying a barrier to reality and a metaphor for existence in a twilight zone.

Spivak, the leading feminist critique, cites the examples of widows burnt at the pyre of the husband in her essay. She emphasized the condition of women who are doubly oppressed–firstly by patriarchy and secondly by colonialism. Leela Gandhi says:

By 'Subaltern' Spivak meant the oppressed subject, the members of Antonio Gramsci's subaltern classes or more generally those of inferior rank and her question followed on the work began in the early 1980s by a collection of individuals now known as Subaltern Studies group. The stated objective of this group was to promote a systematic and informed discussion of Subaltern themes in the field of South Asian Studies. Further they described their project as an attempt to study the general attribute of subordination in South Asian Society whether this is expressed in terms of class, caste, age, gender and office or in any other way. Fully alert to the complex ramification arising from the composition of subordination, the Subaltern studies group sketched out its wide-ranging concern both with the visible history, politics, economics and sociology of subalternity and with the occluded attitudes, ideologies and belief systems- in short, the cultural informing that condition. (1-2)

Edward Said's work on *Orientalism* is related to the idea of the subaltern. It explains the way in which Orientalism produced the foundation and the justification for the domination of the '*Other*' through colonialism. The Europeans, Said argues, created an imagined geography of the Orient before the European exploration through predefined images of savage and monstrous places that lay outside of the known world. The imagined geography eventually consolidated the physical geography. During initial exploration of the Orient these mythologies were reinforced as travelers brought back reports of monsters and strange lands. The idea of difference and strangeness of the Orient continued to be perpetuated through media and discourse creating an "us" and "them" binary through which Europeans defined them by defining the differences of the Orient. This laid the foundation for colonialism by presenting the Orient as primitive and irrational and therefore in need of help to become modern in the European sense. The discourse of Orientalism is Eurocentric and does not seek to include the voices of the Orientals themselves, "The relationship between Occident and Orient is a relationship of power, of domination, of varying degrees of complex hegemony" (5-6).

Since its very beginning the subaltern historiography which emerged in the 1980s, resulted into a major transition in South Asian historiography and posed a vigorous challenge to existing historical scholarship. It was largely by its relentless postcolonial critique that Indian history came to be seen in a different life. Indian History had thus found a new approach that was so critically needed. The Nationalist and the Cambridge Schools became the focus of their criticism due to their elite based analysis of history. They also contested the Marxist School due to the fact that their mode of production-based narratives has a tendency of merging inevitably into the nationalist ideology of modernity and progress. Moreover, the Subalterns rightly pointed out that the Marxist found it really difficult to accept the ideology of caste and religion as crucial factors in Indian History, which to them was somewhat backward and degrading. They were thus, according to the Subalterns, totally unable to gather vital historical data from lived experiences of various oppressed classes, which were submerged in religious and social customs.

Ranajit Guha is undoubtedly the most famous name among all Subaltern Historians. His *Elementary Aspects of Peasants Insurgency in Colonial India* is considered to be the most powerful example of Subaltern historical book. By returning to the 19th century peasants' insurrection in Colonial India he offered a fascinating account of the peasants' insurgent consciousness, rumors, mystic visions, religiosity and bonds of community. In this interesting account, Guha attempted to uncover the true face of peasants' existence in colonial India. In one place he pointed out that the peasants were denied recognition as a subject of history in his own right even for a subject that was all his own. Elitist historiographies were unable to put the peasants' conditions and their insurgency in correct perspective as they could not go beyond limitations that were characteristic of their historiographical institution.

He claimed that there existed in colonial India an 'autonomous' domain of the 'politics of people' that was organized differently than the politics of the elite.

This is a sense summed up the entire argument put forward by subaltern thinkers. Peasant uprisings in colonial India, he argued, reflected a separate and autonomous grammar of mobilization in its most comprehensive form. The landlords, the money lenders and the colonial government officials formed a composite apparatus of dominance over the peasants. Their exploitation according to Guha was primarily political in character and economic exploitation, so upheld and stressed by the other schools, mainly the Marxist was mainly one of its several instances.

The subaltern studies aimed at promoting the study and discussion of the subaltern themes in South Asian Studies. The principal aim was to rectify the elitist bias found in most of the academic works in South Asian Studies. Guha believed that the politics of the subalterns did not constitute an autonomous domain, for it originated from elite politics nor did its existence depend on the latter. Subordination in its various forms has always been the central focus of the Subaltern studies. But throughout subsequent chapters the whole concept of subalternity underwent various shifts. The essays of the subsequent volumes reflect divergence in interest, motives and theories. But in spite of these shifts, one aspect of the Subaltern Studies has remained unchanged. It is an effort to see and rethink history from the perspective of the Subalterns and to give them their due in the historical process. The new contributors ended up giving new form and substance subalternity.

The last two decades of the twentieth century have witnessed the emergence of diverse themes within the subaltern historiographical school. Historians have noticed that the later volumes of the Subaltern Studies were dominated by the desire to analyze the portrayal of subalternity by the dominant discourses. Apart from these volumes a number of books appeared in the decades of 80s and 90s. Historian, Partha Chatterjee made notable contributions in this respect. His works proved crucial at this juncture to understand that engagement with elite themes is not altogether new to the subalterns.

A number of earlier essays has revolved around these themes during the formative years, most important among them being Ranajit Guha's *Prose of Counter Insurgency.* The difference in the later essays lies in the fact that while the earlier works wanted to establish the subalterns as subjects of their own history, the latter works concentrated on various aspects of dominance confronted by the Subaltern sections. They also shed new lights on the domains of culture and politics of the period and their roles in the whole picture.

These writings have been able to outline the whole process of history being written from the point of view of elite nationalism and their limitations. In this respect Shahid Amin's *Gandhi as Mahatma, Approvers Testimony* and *Judicial Discourse: The Case of Chouri Choura* isworth-reading. Communalism also emerged as a significant theme in Subaltern writings of 90s. Gyan Pandey has some notable works to his credit about the Hindu Muslims riots in modern India. This theme has become all the more important with the resurgence of Hindu and Muslim fundamentalism in the recent times. Historian Gyan Prakash in one of his essays said that the real significance of the shift to the analysis of discourses is the reformulation of the notion of subaltern.

The decade of the 80s assumes a special significance because the fact of caste, gender, and religion become important reference points in history writing. Subaltern history in particular understood the need to document the lives of all the oppressed people, like peasants and workers, tribals and lower caste women and dalits, whose voices were seldom heard thus excluded from the canon of history. Subaltern school has no doubt made great contribution in the realm of Indian historiography. But nevertheless, it is not totally free from shortcomings. Sumit Sarkar in his famous essay "The Decline of the Subaltern" in his book *Writing Social History* states:

Subaltern studies do not happen to be the first Indian historiographical school whose reputation has come to be evaluated primarily in terms of audience response in the west for many Indian readers, particularly those getting interested in postmodern trends for the first time. The sense of being 'with it' strongly conveyed by Subaltern Studies appears far more important than any possible insubstantiality of empirical consent. Yet some eclectic borrowings or verbal similarities apart, the claim (or ascription) of being postmodern is largely spurious, in which ever since we might want to deploy that ambiguous and self-consciously polysemic term. (103)

Thus, the representation of the subaltern has always been problematic and complicated by their position in literature, politics and history. Indian feminist deconstructive critic Gayatri Chakravorty Spivak suggests in her book *In Other Worlds: Essays in Cultural Politics* (1988) that the phased development of the subaltern is complicated by the imperialist project. At the same time Morten is of the view:

She attempts to formulate a critical vocabulary that is appropriate to describe the experiences and histories of particular individuals and social groups who are historically repressed and exploited by the European colonialism. (Morton 47)

For Spivak words like 'the colonized', 'woman', and 'the worker' may seem to provide a coherent political identity for disempowered individuals and groups to unite against the oppressors. These master signifiers do not do any justice to the lives and histories of those people who were frequently ignored and subsequently forgotten by anti-colonial national independence movements. Against such master signifiers, Spivak proposes to use the word subaltern to conceptualize a range of different subject positions which are not predefined by dominant political discourses. As Spivak claims in an interview published in *Polygraph:*

I like the word 'subaltern' for one reason. It is truly situational. Subaltern began as a description of a certain rank in the military. The word subaltern used under censorship of Gramsci: he called Marxism 'monism,' and was obliged to call the proletarian 'subaltern.' That word, used under duress, has been transformed into the description of everything that doesn't fall under strict class analysis. I like that because it has no theoretical rigor. (Spivak 141)

If we look at Spivak's formulation carefully, we are able to understand that people or the groups who are marginalized, who cannot raise their voice collectively and have no political consciousness are 'subalterns'. The task of understanding who they are, therefore, is crucial for understanding the politics of subaltern representation.

The social order of any society should be built on the social consciousness. It is well established that the dominant ideology determines the social consciousness of the society. The social consciousness of the society, by its very nature, excludes the real agonies of the people. There are many theories about consciousness. Self-consciousness is being conscious of something correlated to one's life; in this sense, consciousness means knowing oneself or understanding the surrounding of our own.

Consciousness always involves an object of consciousness. Perhaps subjects learn about something when they direct their attention to it, making it an object of consciousness. Everyone has consciousness of what he possesses, but until they create a general code of conduct it is impossible to create a general will on the problems they face. So, the self-awareness and consciousness on the part of the degraded and marginalized societies become essential in order to resist the situations which produce the degradation they suffer from.

By the use of philosophical and religious texts, rituals, festivals and art forms, the dominant group suppresses other cultural and religious expressions and parallel objects that belong to the communities other than the dominant group. Actually, the folklores of the world and especially those of India were either distorted or marginalized to serve the interests of the dominant group. By and by the subaltern notion or consciousness of the working people who used to or were forced to create all beauties of the world gets degraded or marginalized. The primary dominating sectors of the society like governance and education facilitated the upper class to hold and practice their social order in every sphere of life. As a result, a large number of people were forced to remain in the backyards of the socio-economic and political progress. The dominant group enjoys superior status in the realm of culture and politics. This hierarchy is clearly visible in the Indian social order where "subaltern classes" remain as a mere means to attain the wealth and power for the leisure/superior class.

The hierarchy based on birth is a social concept that people used to take it for granted as reality without questioning its legitimacy. The caste and ethnic system is so closed that the interaction among these castes are restricted in the name of purity by the upper class. The upper class/caste used the 'caste ideology' as a means to secure their political and economic power and sustain their domination in the society. The compartmentalization of caste is so perfect that the populace from the lower strata/caste failed to share their feelings, etiquettes rationale etc., and thus unable to generate and share protests against the ruling social order.

The intellectuals, as defined by the Italian thinker Antonio Gramsci, play an important role in the creation and maintenances of social orders. They create the world based on their own ideas, where they placed man in different caste/social categories. The 'mental servitude', accordingly is made possible by the ideology of the dominant group which acts as hegemonic power in the society. Here, the 'hegemonic power' means the ruling ideology which knowingly or unknowingly subjugates all other groups and their visions.

The hegemonic ideology keeps up a social order based on purity of the upper castes. Gramsci defined hegemony as the consent produced in any society by the organization of civil society, contrary to the state with its apparatus of coercive power. The hegemony within civil society supports the leading group's authority over political society. This is supported by the juridical apparatus of the political society that protects the dominant group's hegemony within civil society through coercive measures. In this sense, the integral state comprises not only political society and civil society, but it also includes dictatorship and hegemony. In basis terms, hegemony is protected by coercion and coercion is protected by hegemony, and these together protect the dominant group's political and economic positions.

Since the contemporary society has been witnessing new awareness and new readings, the social consciousness and mobility among the subaltern are also increasing. The new awareness and consciousness will dismantle the hegemony and assert the genuine nature of the living culture. In other words, the consciousness of the subaltern will replace a dominant culture by a living culture and convince the society about the plight of the majority in the history of the Indian society. The subaltern consciousness means the consciousness about oneself and realizing the hegemony. It is simultaneously the consciousness to protect one's own history and to resist the domination of the other. As in the philosophy of Husserl it is the 'life world' of the subaltern. The consciousness of the subaltern is a pre-condition before attaining class consciousness. To be class conscious, one should become a citizen of the public sphere. The emancipation of the marginalized communities in India depends upon the extent of recovering the consciousness of the subaltern from the depths of their own history.

Subalternity is a kind of subordinate and exterior positionality in relation to a hegemonic power relation, a relation that is constituted by and operates through both structural power and the normalized forms of knowledge and subjectivity of those who participate in it. Subalterns are disempowered and expelled by the hegemonic relation because they do not speak within the terms of its form of problematization and its rules for legitimate consent and dissent. It is not that the subaltern cannot speak, but they cannot speak within the terms of the hegemonic relation, or in a way that is legible or recognizable to the hegemony, or at least not immediately so. However, subalternity is a positionality or moment in relation to hegemony. In this way practices, subjectivities, knowledge, and normativities can be subalternized, but each can also be subalternized in full or in part, depending on the constitution of the hegemonic relation itself, and in relation to multiple crisscrossing hegemonies.

Subaltern v/s Diaspora

The link between "diaspora" and "subaltern" is complex. The people of diaspora were settlers, migrants, transported convicts, slaves, or labourers. The culture produced by diaspora cannot contain so many resonances of the movement—the imagination of their homelands, sense of tradition, the circumstances of their removal and their sense of shame if acknowledging their bond with their homeland. Indeed, life like this is a Janus-like journey looking backward while moving forward. Janus being a Roman god having two faces, one looking forward and one back, implies the ambivalent nature of the diaspora.

Since long history has witnessed the mass migration of the people of Indian sub-continent to different countries making Indian Diaspora as the oldest and the largest in magnitude. It enjoys an air of importance in the global scenario. Studies have revealed that the single largest ethnic community is comprised of people of Indian origin in Fiji (49%), Guyana (53%), Mauritius (74%), Trinidad and Tobago (40%) and Surinam (37%).

In Asian countries like Hong Kong, Malaysia, Singapore, Sri Lanka, South Africa and East Africa; people of Indian origin form substantial minority communities. In Australia, Canada, the United Kingdom and the United States of America, the people of Indian origin are of significant number. Indian diaspora has thus evolved out as unique wave reaching every nook and corner of the globe having almost unique socio-cultural histories and being subjected to different economic and political situations, the Indian communities abroad have evolved as distinct diasporic entities. They are nevertheless Indian as they manifest in varying degrees.

These immigrants, whatever their reason for migration be, financial, social, political, no matter whether they migrated for trade and commerce, as religious preachers, as labourers, convicts, soldiers, as expatriates or refugees, exiles (forced or voluntary), or as guest workers in search of better life and opportunities have shared some common things as well as differences which are based on their conditions of migration and period of stay in the adopted land. Mostly the migrants suffer from the pain of being far from their homes, the memories of their motherland and the anguish of leaving behind everything familiar agonizes the minds of migrants. Thus, due to change of location and position these immigrants became subaltern in foreign land. William Safran has observed, "They continue to relate personally or vicariously, to the homeland in a way or another, and their ethnic-communal consciousness and solidarity are importantly defined by the existence of such a relationship" (Safran 23).

Immigrant experiences are a composite one made up of journeys and border crossings. Migration leads to separation. Separation means rebirth in a country marked by new culture and new adjustments in an alien land. Immigrant psyche shows the interaction of traditional culture within the culture of an adopted land and in this way brings about a transformation in the inherited tradition and culture of the immigrant. Aggression interrupted tension and expectant confusion have become the formative narratives of their writings.

These diaspora people, on becoming subaltern, oscillate between two mutually exclusive worlds. Diaspora may be termed as transitional people being in ambivalent space. These diasporas, according to Homi K. Bhabha, tend to move in an obvious circle, i.e., from home culture to alien culture leading to an assimilated culture. Edward W. Said also adds to the definition and classification of Diasporas:

The person who finds his homeland sweet is still a tender beginner, he to whom every soil is as his native one is already strong, but he is perfect to whom the entire world is a foreign place and a survival in fact is about the connection between things. (*Culture and Imperialism* 407)

The contribution and combination of the two cultural traditions have made literature an interesting piece of art with their expression of shared experiences. In subaltern studies the diasporic literature witnessed different types of cultural values, aspects, mode of living, language, attire, religion, housement and un-housement. It aims at certain cross-cultural issues that create a ‘third space’ of all the nationalities and geographical boundaries.

Diasporic subjects must keep a collective memory of their past and keep their links with the mother land alive so that they can qualify for a Diasporas identity. Roots are very important, but when they prevent people from adjusting to new and endlessly changing condition, they may become chaotic. Therefore, it might be a fundamental notion for Diaspora writers that they need to be conscious in depicting the details about their homelands. It is obvious that the diaspora condition can be rather dynamic and ambivalent, and could be interpreted with paradoxical conditions of alienation from the host society and co-exists with a sense of belongingness.

An expatriate writer is not only a man who travels across the physical boundaries; rather his imagination, culture, psyche, sociology and anthropology also travel with him, causing a sort of perpetual conflict of fluid identity and alternative centers. According to Jayaram, the immigrants carry with them:

A socio-cultural baggage which among other things consists of (a) a predefined social identity, (b) a set of religious beliefs and practices, (c) a framework of norms and values governing family and kinship organization, and food habits and (d) language. (16)

In this way subaltern consciousness in the world of literature has become an increasingly dominant phenomenon when we deal subaltern in diasporic location. It is the mental flight of people constantly trying to reconstruct their present from a past that haunts them repeatedly. All such attempts, however, are liable to flounder as their own roots re-assert their peculiarities. Their roots strike against a frozen and fractured consciousness forcing them to begin search for locating the originality that can warmly encapsulate their ambivalent identities. The search of the emigrant for a permanent foothold is the starting point of diaspora literature for subaltern people.

The worldwide culture, economic and political changes resulted in the emergence of diaspora writing by the prominent writers such as Derek Wolcott, Margaret Atwood, Michael Ondaatje, Neil Bissoondath, M. G. Vassanji and V. S. Naipaul. These writers represented the generation that had to encounter the struggle that resulted from the withdrawal of imperial order and the resultant cultural confusion. Although all the diasporic writers mentioned above hold a sway over the perceptive reader, Naipaul seems to be outstanding among the popular postcolonial novelists due to his exceptional treatment of common diasporic experiences and Trinidadian circumstances. He is an expatriate who has started with no other recourses than his steadfastness and the elegance that he has developed through hard work. For his relatively long stay in England, he has never felt at home and still recognizes himself as an outsider somewhat in a state of subaltern with a diasporic consciousness.

The Indian diaspora is one of the most outstanding and a complex socio-economic pattern. Migration is the phenomenon that has been taking place for millions of years and even prevails today all over the world. When an individual can no longer acquire the necessary resources to sustain themselves at their locations they migrate to a place where the resources are available. In the earlier period, people moved either because of the social and economic condition of the home country or attracted by the images of destination with greater socio-economic opportunities. The Indian Diaspora is:

Like a banyan tree, traditional symbol of the Indian way of life he spreads out its roots in several soils, drawing nourishment from one when the rest dry up. Far from begin homeless, he/she has several homes, and that is the only way he has increasingly come to feel the home in the world. (Jain10)

Since the immigration countries are known for their welfare and social system there is always an attraction to go there. The instinct to migrate can have various reasons. "Migration of people has been transmuted into mobility of individuals" (Park 349).

The Indian diaspora has been formed by a scattering of population not in the Jewish sense, an exodus of population at a particular point of time. This sporadic migration traces a steady pattern if a telescopic view is taken over a period of time: from the indentured labourers of the past to the IT technocrats of the present day. Sudesh Mishra in his essay "From Sugar to Masala" divides the Indian diaspora into two categories - the old and the new. He writes, "This distinction is between, on the one hand, the semi-voluntary flight of indentured peasants to non-metropolitan plantation colonies such as Fiji, Trinidad, Mauritius, South Africa, Malaysia, Surinam, and Guyana, Britain" (Mishra 276).

Especially after Indian independence the Indian diasporic community has acquired a new identity due to the processes of self-fashioning and increasing acceptance by the West. It is interesting to note that the history of diasporic Indian writing is as old as the diaspora itself. In fact, the first Indian writing in English is credited to Dean Mahomed, who was born in Patna, India, and after working for fifteen years in the Bengal Army of the British East India Company, migrated to "eighteenth century Ireland, and then to England" (Nayar xx) in 1784. His book *The Travels of Dean Mahomet* was published in 1794. It predates about forty years the first English text written by an Indian residing in India, Kylas Chunder Dutt's *Imaginary History* published in 1835.

The first Indian English novel was *Rajmohan's Wife* by Bankimchandra Chatterjee, published much later in 1864. It shows that the contribution of the Indian diaspora to Indian writing in English is not new. Interestingly, the descendants of the Indian indentured labourers in the so called "girmit colonies" have predominantly favoured writing in English, the lingua franca of the world. Seepersad Naipaul, Shiva Naipaul, V. S. Naipaul, Amitav Ghosh, Cyril Dabydeen, David Dabydeen, Sam Selvon, M. G. Vassanji, Neil Bissoondath, K. S. Maniam and Rohinton Mistry are significant contributors in the field of diaspora studies.

The novels of theolder generation of diasporic Indian writers like Raja Rao, G. V. Desani, SanthaRama Rau, Balachandra Rajan, Nirad Chaudhuri and Ved Mehta predominantlylook back at India and rarely record their experiences away from India asexpatriates. It is as if these writers have discovered their Indianness when theyare out of India. Obviously, they have the advantage of looking at their homelandfrom the outside. The distance affords them the detachment that is so necessaryto have a clear perception of their native land. In that sense, through their writing,they recreate India:

(T)hat instead of worshipping the leftovers and relics of a now inaccessible homeland as the old diaspora of indentured labourers did, the new diaspora of international Indian English writers live close to their market, in the comforts of the suburbia of advanced capital but draw their raw material from the inexhaustible imaginative resources of that messy and disorderly subcontinent that is India. (Paranjape 252)

These writers record their Indian experiences and even if they look back at their homeland it is often in an elegiac tone rather than with nostalgia. Paranjape explicates this point in considering the novels of Rohinton Mistry. Ultimately Indian writers in the West are increasingly identifying themselves with the literary tradition of the migrant writers of the world. Rushdie says that "Swift, Conrad, Marx, Melville, Hemingway and Bellow are as much our literary forebears as Tagore or Ram Mohan Roy" (20). The modern diasporic Indian writers can be grouped into two distinct classes. One class comprises those who have spent a part of their life in India and have carried the baggage of their native land off shore. The other class comprises those who have been bred since childhood outside India. They have had a view of their country only from the outside as an exotic place of their origin. The writers of the former group have a literal displacement whereas those belonging to the latter group find themselves rootless. Both the groups of writers have produced an enviable corpus of English literature.

These writers while depicting migrant characters in their fiction explore the theme of displacement and self-fashioning. The diasporic Indian writers' depiction of dislocated characters gains immense importance if seen against the geo-political background of the vast Indian subcontinent. That is precisely why such works have a global readership and an enduring appeal. The diasporic Indian writers have generally dealt with characters from their own displaced community but some of them have also taken a liking for Western characters and they have been convincing in dealing with them.

In this way, it can be said without any shade of doubt that Diaspora continually reinvents their circumstances and in doing so they form their own history. The cultural sediment that survives the chain of movements forms the modes of narrative. William Safran has characterized the

Diaspora on the basis of cultural sedimentation:

i. They or their ancestors have been dispersed from a specific original 'centre' to two or more peripheral regions.
v. They retain a collective memory, vision or myth about their original homeland—its physical location, history and achievements.
v. They believe that they are not—and perhaps cannot be fully accepted by their host society and therefore feel partly alienated and insulated from it.
v. They regard their ancestral homeland as their true, ideal home and as the place to which they or their descendants would eventually return— when conditions are appropriate.
v. They believe that they should collectively, be committed to the maintenance or restoration of their homeland and to its safety and prosperity.
v. They continue to relate personally or vicariously to that homeland in one way or the other, and their ethno communal consciousness and solidarity are importantly defined by the existence of such a relationship. (Safran 83-84)

Mishra holds different argument about Diaspora when he says that Safran's characterization takes for granted the existence of an exclusive and pure community whereas Diaspora are the result confluence with the host society and it is the "creation of its own political myths rather than the real possibilities of a return to a homeland," (Mishra70) which is its actual characteristic. In the creation of their own political selves, the Diaspora have pushed issues of nationalism, nation and nationhood to the forefront and have reminded us of what Renan had said about national identity—for a unit to rise and take on the condition of nationhood, it is necessary for all individuals concerned to remember what brings them together and forget what could tear them apart.

In diaspora study the role of nation becomes very important. About nation Anderson says that nation is "an imagined political community." He is of the opinion that the ideas of nationalism are "cultural artifacts of a particular kind" and any attempt to understand these must begin with an understanding of how these ideas "came into historical being" (46). In this way the same ideology and analogy can be extended to a study of the diasporic brand of nationalism.

Having forsaken their homeland for personal benefit, these communities feel responsible towards the home country. An explanation can be found in Homi Bhabha's definition of the "third space" as a hybrid location rich in turmoil from which the inter-subjective and collective experiences of nation, community interest or cultural values are negotiated. Bhabha looks upon these "third space" as "gathering" of scattered people, of "exile and émigrés and refugee, gatherings on the edge of foreign cultures, gathering memories of other worlds lived retroactively; gathering the past in a ritual of revival; gathering the present" (*Nation and Narration* 291).

That is why the formation of diaspora identity is a big step in the larger transformation of the history of the diaspora. If a writer enters an engagement with history, he writes himself book by book into the "hybrid location" that Bhabha speaks of, and then if he goes on, there is a possibility of his writing himself out of the "hybrid location" and achieving a more objective world-view. It is in this sense that this study attempts to read V. S. Naipaul's engagement with the history of India. The question of historical circumstance cannot be washed away just because it is far removed from the present reality. What happens when a third world intellectual stands face-to-face with his historical circumstance? Is it the beginning of further alienation or the assimilation? These questions have manifested themselves in different ways in different writers. At the end of *Culture and Imperialism,* Edward Said attempts an answer by quoting Hugo of St. Victor, "The person who finds his homeland sweet is still a tender beginner; he to whom every soil is as his native one as already strong; but he is perfect to whom the entire world is as foreign place" (407).

Michel Foucault's concept of "heterotopias" when applied to Diaspora reveals a new paradigm. Spaces can be divided into socially or politically constructed binaries as '*other.*' These '*other*' spaces are spaces of crisis, subjugation or colonization. Heterotopias when applied to Diasporas immediately shed its bipolar dimensions and become multipolar. Diaspora being the result of the coming together of the 'own' and the 'other' is not a third space outside the realm of own/other and works towards diluting, shifting and displacing these binaries. It thus succeeds in forming Fanon's third alternative of a change that originates with the "wretched of the earth" leaving aside both bourgeois assimilation and bourgeois nationalism. Works of social scientists, philosophers and historians have influenced the work of interdisciplinary theorists that have been discussed so far. The theory of Diaspora traverses these interdisciplinary theories; it seeks to achieve that balance in remembering and forgetting which was advocated by Renan. But problem does not end there. The trouble is not only in deciding what to forget but also, to paraphrase. It is a battle to decide who will imagine the community.

Thus, in subaltern study, Diaspora refers to a matrix of political and social concerns whose interdependence needs to be analyzed and studied to combat the tensions that are tearing at the humanitarian values of the worlds and exposing societies to extreme traumas. At the onset a distinction needs to be made between the uprooted intellectuals' writers and the nameless uprooted masses. Next a distinction needs to be made within the former category on the basis of circumstance; those moving for reasons of intellectual affinity, those escaping oppression in their homeland, political dissidents and the waifs of colonialism.

In an interview with Nikhil Padgaonkar for Doordarshan, Edward W. Said reflected on the condition of exile:

I think that if one is an intellectual, one has to exile oneself from what has been given to you, what is customary, and to see it from a point of view that looks at it as if it were something that is provisional and foreign to oneself. That allows for independence—commitment—but independence and a certain kind of detachment. (Said 13)

Naipaul discusses the issues of dislocations, migrations, exile, the idea of being unanchored and displaced, and the enigma of a displaced coolie. Naipaul is known for last three decades as a writer of exile, the writer in search of home. An important theme of his books is paradox of freedom. Naipaul's fictional world is located in the interplay of realistic external situations and personal lives. He writes about democracy, freedom and independence in an ironic style. He presents his view of history as a complex interaction between the individual and circumstances, the collective slave and separate individual, the exploiter and the exploited, the slavery and colonialism. He got Bennet Award in 1980. William Walsh pays a rich tribute to Naipaul's genius in the following words:

> He is engaged with the stress and strains we recognize as crucial in our experience now. His writing is nervous and present, this, together with the mixture in him of creeds, cultures and continents, with his expatriate career, his being able to practice an art in and of totally dissimilar worlds, all gives him a peculiarly contemporary quality. (Walsh 1)

Doubly Marginalized Space in Double Diaspora Location

In the present global scenario, subaltern theme has become so prominent that it is regularly used in various disciplines such as history, sociology, psychology and literature. Subaltern literature reflects various themes such as oppression, marginalization, gender discrimination, subjugation of lower and working classes, neglected sections of society and deprived classes etc. In the context of globalization 'Third World' countries are encountering the state of poverty and oppression. Subaltern literature is one of the subdivisions of postcolonialism.

With the advent of globalization, the boundaries have become more and more blurred. These boundaries provide opportunity to live and work in other parts of the world. This significant moving in and moving out of people occurs not only from developing countries to developed countries but also from one developed country to another, as well as between developing countries. Since the diaspora has become a global phenomenon and human beings are always at the centre of such diasporic movements. It is essential to look into the lives and problems of such migrants to identify the alienation and problems of the people who have become a part of the diaspora.

To deal with subaltern consciousness has been a favorite theme of expatriate writers. Different postcolonial themes like the theme of identity crisis, fractured/torn-identities, East-West encounters, rejection, anxiety, love-hate relationship within two cultures, homelessness, migration, expatriation, displacement, uprooting from the homeland, belongingness, cultural adaption, political insurgency, the feeling of 'no whereness' etc., reflecting subaltern and diasporic ambivalence are projected in the writings of Naipaul and his contemporaries like Neil Bissoondath and M.G. Vassanji.

The Indian expatriate has its origin in the abolition of slavery in Trinidad in 1834. The emancipated slaves refused to work on the fields on the predefined conditions. These immigrant workers were imported from Portugal, France, Africa, Madeira, the United States and China as well as from the smaller islands of the Caribbean, but the main supplier of labour was India. The shift of population between the colonies resulted into the formation of heterogeneous multicultural societies. Gayatri Spivak truly and elaborately comments upon the diasporic Indians:

Over the centuries we had histories of indentured labour being taken to the Afro-Caribbean. After the change of regimes in certain African nations, Indians moved from, Africa, then to Britain; then Indians in waves in the early 60's, professional Indians, went to the United State as part of the brain-drain. These Indians who are spread out over the world, for different kinds of historical reasons, they are diasporic. (59)

Many Indians migrated to West Indies Caribbean Island in the late nineteenth century as indentured labourers in the sugarcane fields were the major displacement for those who settled in Trinidad as a separate ethnic group but are still sticking to their native cultural identities. The first Indian immigrants as indentured labourers arrived in Port of Spain on 30 May, 1845. When immigration from India was banned, near about one lac fifty thousand labourers had settled in Trinidad. Most of them came from U.P. and Bihar. In an essay David Ormerod narrates:

The indenture scheme is still remembered with bitterness. Trinidad Indians is convinced that they occupy their particular spot on the earth's surface because their forefathers were duped by the planters and the recruiting agents. Conditions were misrepresented. (171)

The present population of Trinidad consists of people of Amerindians and the descendants of the people of three continents—Europe, Africa and Asia—who have made these island their uneasy home. Only this confused amalgam of races remains as a witness to the forlorn history of the region.

The expatriates were forced to live among heterogeneous groups formed by the Africans, native Trinidadians and other displaced groups tormented by the colonizers in one way or the other. For expatriate, the urge to survive becomes the immediate requirement. Their displacement from traditional culture left a deep scar on the psyche of the colonized people as in the alien land they found themselves in the painful state of betweenity—constantly searching for an identity and home. It was nothing but the impact of colonization on the minds of the displaced. Bit by bit they are robbed of their originality. Due to this displacement of people from their native land to alien land for one reason or the other, the term "diaspora" came into vogue.

Because of this continual sense of dislocation, the colonized people were made to suffer not only in their native land where they were born but also in the alien land where they were forced to migrate because of economic and political compulsions. It is in this sense that diaspora acquires a universal connotation that indeed transcends the boundaries both—temporal and spatial ones. Though the term diaspora has always attracted the intellectual attention, it has gained intense currency in the postcolonial era. It is so because postcolonial anguish appears to be inextricably intertwined with the diasporic angst among the people inhabiting in the Third World.

The dilemmas of developing a national identity to counter the colonial rule figure prominently in the writings of the postcolonial writers who seek to articulate and even celebrate the indigenous cultural identities. The primary concern of the postcolonial literature is to study the experiences of people who happened to live in colonized countries.

The life long quest for past and involuntary assimilation into the alien culture gave way to an important concept in postcolonial theory popularly termed as "ambivalence". *Webster's New World College Dictionary* defines the term as "simultaneous conflicting feelings toward a person or thing, as love and hate" (43). The ambivalence gives rise to in-betweenness, half-ness, dichotomies, dilemmas and divided-selves of the colonial natives and expatriates. This ambivalent tendency among concepts like "mimicry", "hybridity", "creolization" and "multiculturalism" prevail in the colonial / postcolonial

Third World.

Some important and broad concepts associated to postcolonial studies include—the formation of empire, the impact of colonization on postcolonial history, economy, science and culture. The thinkers / critics like Frantz Fanon, Edward W. Said, George Lamming, Terry Eagleton, Homi K. Bhabha, Ania Loomba, Leela Gandhi, Gayatri Spivak, Bill Ashcroft and Ashis Nandy, to name only a few, have spelled out their varied interpretation of this diasporic phenomenon which gets reflected in some of the key concepts such as colonialism, postcolonialism, and cultural hegemony.

Works Cited

Beauvoir, Simon De. "The Mother." *French Feminism Reader*. Ed. Kelly Oliver. Lanham: Rowman, 2000. Print.

Bhabha, Homi. *Nation and Narration*. London: Routledge, 1990. Print.

---. *Location of Culture*. London: Rutledge, 1994. Print.

Fanon, Frantz. *Black Skin, White Masks*. New York: Grove Press, 1967. Print.

Foucault, Michel. *The Archaeology of Knowledge*. New York: Pantheon, 1972. Print.

Gandhi, Leela. *Postcolonial Theory: A Critical Introduction*. New Delhi: Oxford University Press, 1998. Print.

Guha, Ranajit. "On Aspects of the Historiography of Colonial India." *Mapping*

Subaltern Studies and the Postcolonial. Ed. Vinayak Chaturvedi. London: Verso, 2000. Print.

---. ed. *Subaltern Studies: Writings on South Asian History and Society* (7 Volumes). Delhi: OUP, 1982. Print.

--- . ed. *Subaltern Studies II:* The Prose of Counter Insurgency.Delhi: OUP, 1982. Print.

--- . *Elementary Aspects of Peasant Insurgency in Colonial India*. Delhi: OUP, 1983. Print.

Hall, Stuart. "Cultural Identity and Diaspora." *Theorizing Diaspora: A Reader*. Ed.

Jana Evan Braziel and Anita Mannur. London: Blackwell Publishing Ltd, 2003.

Jain, Jasbir. "Problems of Postcolonial Literatures." *Problems of Postcolonial Literatures and Other Essays*. Ed. Jain Jasbir. Jaipur: Printwell, 1991. 1-15.

Mishra, Vijay. "New Lamps for Old: Diasporas Migrancy Border." *Commonwealth*

Writing: A Study in Expatriate Experience. Eds. R. K. Dhawan and L.S.R. Krishna Sastry. New Delhi: Prestige Books, 1994. Print.

Morton, Stephen. *Gayatri Chakravarty Spivak*. Oxon: Routledge, 2003. Print.

Mustapha, Nasser. "The Influence of Indian Islam on Fundamentalist Trends in Trinidad and Tebogo." *The Indian Diaspora: Dynamics of Migration*. Ed. N. Jayaram. New Delhi: Sage Publication, 2004. Print.

Ormerod, David. "In a Derelict Land." *Critical Perspective on V. S. Naipaul*. Ed. R.D. Hammer. Washington D. C.: Three Continents Press, 1977. Print.

Paranjape, Makarand. "Triple Ambivalence: Australia, Canada, and South Asia in the Diasporic Safran, William. "Diaspora in Modern Societies: Myths of Homeland and Return." *Diaspora: A Journal of Transnational Studies* 1.1 (1991): 12-18.

Said, Edward. "Two Visions in Heart of Darkness." *Culture and Imperialism* (1993): 22-31. *Pdf*. Web. 04 Sep. 2012.

--- . *Culture and Imperialism*. London: Vintage, 1994. Print.

Sarkar, Sumit, ed. “The Decline of the Subaltern.” *Writing Social History*. Delhi: OUP, 1997. Print.

Spivak, Gayatri Chakravorti. *In Other Worlds: Essays in Cultural Politics*. New York: Routledge, 1987. Print.

Young, Robert. *Post- Colonialism: A Very Short Introduction*. New York: Oxford University Press, 2003. Print.

CHAPTER ONE

Gendered Subalternism in A House for Mr. Biswas and Half a Life

The women in the postcolonial society are doubly marginalized. However, in the hierarchy of structural oppression, there are women who are placed further down the scale. Tribal, lower-caste, differently-abled, lesbian and lower-class women all come at the lower end of the hierarchy system. Writings by such women often present a challenge to feminists because they resist homogenizing into the larger category of Third World Women. Every text in subaltern writing functions as a collective document, as the narrative moves from individual to community through a re-telling of trauma. Aboriginal writing from Australia, Canada and South America are also kinds of postcolonial testomonia.

Perhaps the most important example of the genre is Regoberta Menchu's *I, Rigoberta Menchu* (1984), a text which has attained cult status as *testimonio.* Menchu, a Quiche Mayan woman from Guatemala, documented the traumatic events of her community. Her opening paragraph states:

My name is Rigonerta Menchu. I am twenty-three years. This is testimony, I'd like to stress that it's not only my life; it's also the testimony of my people. The important thing is that what has happened to me has happened to many other people too . . .. My personal experience is the reality of a whole people. (1)

It becomes the document of a struggle of the entire community and race. Likewise, Bama described her *Karukku* in this way:

The story told in Karukku was not my story alone. It was the depiction of a collective trauma—of my community-whose length cannot be measured in time. I just tried to freeze it forever in one book so that there will be something physical to remind people of the atrocities committed on a section of the society for ages. (http://www.ambedkar.org.)

The linkage between gender and nation becomes more problematic in the case of a diasporic women writer since, as Ania Loomba points out, "If the nation is an imagined community, that imagining is 'profoundly gendered" (215). Thus, once political independence has been gained, women, who have fought the same nationalistic battle with and alongside the men, are sent into the kitchens. Their feminine duties must be resumed in the nation-state. In fact, nothing has changed, as Morgan seems to suggest, "The nation and gender are interlinked social phenomena. Women are 'involved' in or rather delegated the responsibility for, the 'biological' and cultural reproduction of the nation" (Davis 86).

The idea of the nation and the history of nationalism are closely aligned with the history of manliness and manhood. In national struggle women are reduced to supporting roles—basically as keeping the home ready for warrior – nationalistic to return while men did the 'active' work. She becomes the repository of cultural wisdom and morality—and it is her duty to ensure the reproduction of the nation. George Mosse, in fact, argues that "nationalism evolved parallel to modern masculinity" (Nagel 159). Terms such as 'honour', 'patrotism', and 'duty' are masculinized. "Women are sacrificed in the larger interest of the nation" (Nayar 122).

In the fiction of a Caribbean authors such as Michelle Cliff or Jamaica Kincaid, this 'rootedness' in a racial/ethnic and national identity often becomes a quest. Frequently, the quest becomes a negotiation with the past—with their individual, familial, and cultural histories. How women writers engage with their heritage is a significant theme in postcolonial literature. In gender-identity question is mingled with the heritage—identity question.

Thus, Gendered subalternism is created and burdened with the subordinated dimensions always on the right side of the binary oppositions. The subaltern is imbued with the negatives at all levels, be it social, cultural, sexual or personal. The subaltern is the one who is denied an authentic presence. {H}he is the one bereft of voice or dignity: one who is a mere zero, a cipher with no essential meaning or a sense of being. The gravity of the situation is intensified when the subaltern is a woman. She is even denied a subject position. Being at the precarious juncture and crisscrossed by multiple forces of oppression, she is the one who occupies the lowest position in the social ladder. Her presence is not even authenticated; if at all it is done, it is only to enforce the superiority of the male counterpart. She is the deviant, the deform and signifying all the lacks.

Stuart Hall points out the power of discourse to create and reinforce Western dominance. The colonialist discourses describe how Europe represents differences between *'itself'* and *'others'* using European cultural categories, languages and ideas, and performs cultural *Othering*. The knowledge produced by a discourse puts into practice and then becomes reality. "By producing a discourse of difference Europe was able to maintain its dominance over "the other" thereby creating a subaltern by excluding the other from the production of the discourse" (Hall 157). The scenario is the same when the subaltern, particularly the subaltern woman is being represented in mainstream discourse by elite community. It only furthers and reinforces her subalternity. Adopting mainstream discourses to subaltern female experiences only lead to further marginalization of the subalterns both as individuals and as a community.

The predicament of the female subaltern is the most miserable of all oppressive states. It is a lethal combination for the subaltern to be a woman. Her life, dreams, hopes and the basis right to a dignified survival are thwarted by multiple forces of oppression. She is a victim of racism, classism, and most importantly, of the primarily subjugating ideology of patriarchy. The dream of transcending the threatening powers of oppression rather remains elusive for her. Even more pathetic is the fact that the dominant powers have so naturalized the subjugation of women that she often fails to recognize the pitfall that she is in. She wails in that dungeon forever, often taking it as her ordained destiny to be always the erratic, the aberrant and the abnormal.

Feminist literature has constantly endeavored to bring to the limelight the common experience of oppression shared by women. It is significantly laden with ideological gravity and with the nuances of politically laden discourses, exemplifying the axiom, the personal is the political. Feminists down the centuries have dissected and thoroughly verified the category called the feminine. Gender equations become a major area of feminist concern since they regard gender as a cultural construct. Being a woman may be a biological categorization but being feminine is a cultural construct. The category called the feminine is constructed with reference to the male, the masculine, the norm, the centre. "Just as for the ancients there was an absolute vertical with reference to which the oblique is defined, so there is an absolute human type, the masculine" (Beauvoir 15). Simone de Beauvoir further elaborates the process of cultural *Othering*.

The ideology of patriarchy tends to reinforce an already entrenched system of exploitation. Gender equations attain threatening dimensions within the framework of patriarchal dominance. Juliet Michell sees patriarchy as a dominant feature with cultural rooting and maintained through the operation of ideology. It is perpetuated through a process by which subjectivity is culturally constructed. Gendered subjectivity can be seen as "constituted ideologically, ensuring the continuous reproduction of dominant masculinity and dominated femininity" (Michell 197). Patriarchy is not merely an ideology; it is a set of organized power structures with the key positions occupied by man or his supporting mechanism.

Women have been textually constructed according to socially and politically determined norms. Female identity is seen to be impressionable. While men are being, women are continually becoming. The various institutions in society make sure that women fit in the framework of gender roles. Women are continually engaged in the process of becoming something or someone else in order to suit the prevailing notions of what the "real" woman should be like. The media is the space where these notions find free expressions.

Theorizing the subalterns is a disservice as it dilutes the political content of their oppressive experiences. A subaltern account of experience is a construct of oppression and the subaltern needs to articulate is an art of necessity: an art essential for the survival of the individual as well as the community.

The process of indoctrination starts right from childhood. There is even now a categorization of toys as boys' toys which include gun, car and so on and girls' toys predominantly represented by dolls of different types and hues. It is still possible to find playthings labeled in much the same way as in the nineteenth century verse, part of a collection for school boys during their leisure hours at boarding school. Susan Greenhalgh quotes the dialogue in her essay on growing up:

Mamma and Miss Ann
Mamma: Go and buy a Toy, Ann
Ann: I can buy a gun.
Mamma: A gun is not fit for you, Ann.
Ann: Why is a gun not fit for me?
Mamma: A gun is only fit for a boy.
Ann: May I buy a top?
Mamma: No, but you may buy a mop. (Greenhalgh 22)

The fact that this dialogue is targeted in the first instance at a boy underline how vital it is for boys as well as for girls to recognize appropriate conduct since this will ensure that they keep to their own gender roles. The writer in the above lines analyses the roles of male and female in a patriarchal society. It promotes not only the gender stereotype but also creates a myth of masculinity as V. Geetha admits:

A little boy who dashes up a tree, while his sister hovers uncertainly on the ground; an older man plunges in to a life of adventure and travel while his wife or mother anxiously awaits at home hoping and praying for his safety. (127)

In myth of masculinity, powerful images of gender roles or myths of them have been created during the history and "these roles are always socially constructed. Perhaps the most important and embraced role played by humans is the sexual role" (Stuteville 10). Throughout the history, gender roles have been differentiated from each other because of the need of reinforcing gender role responsibilities in society. "The role of males outside the home and females within the home has built a basis for powerful cultural ethics and social norms" (Lin and Yeh 74). Different roles and status positions within a society are influenced by social organizations and rules that vary between cultures. Still, people from all kinds of cultural backgrounds pattern their behavior and consumption based on role norms of their respective sexes. As one of the critics observes:

Therefore, sex or gender can be defined as the activity of managing situated conduct based on normative conceptions of different attitudes and activities that are appropriate for one's sex category. On the other hand, gender can be understood as a cultural distinction that divides power between men and women. (Pronger 280)

The distinction of power between men and women can be seen as the basis for sexual mythology. According to Pronger, sexual mythology is based on the idea that sex is differentiated from gender. Gender relations are seen as "relational and hierarchical – existing social structures define men as the opposite of women but they also see men's social role as masculine principle of domination" (Wörsching 203). The expression of masculine has been used to define the exertion of power and at the same time femininity is connected to the state of disempowerment. This kind of fundamental structuring of patriarchal power proves that gender can be understood as a myth that justifies, expresses and supports the power of men over women.

Traditionally, the only way of seeing men and masculinity has been the myth of hegemonic masculinity. Hegemonic masculinity can be described as "culturally idealized form of particular masculine character" (Connell 89). Masculinity comes hegemonic when it is widely accepted in a culture and when this acceptance strengthens the dominant gender ideal of a certain culture. "Hegemonic masculinity indicates a certain model of masculinity that operates on the terrain of common sense and conventional morality and defines what it means to be a man" (Hanke 235).

The traditional idea of hegemonic masculinity, "the real man", is always told based on the power relationship between men and women. According to Brannon, the real man must never resemble women or display strongly stereotyped feminine characteristics. Physically, real men have "deep voices, they tend to avoid use of cosmetics and they do not usually give much attention to their appearance, clothes and hygiene" (Alexander 545). Being a man requires not being effeminate in physical appearance or mannerism. Additionally, "hegemonic masculinity includes power defined as in terms of physical force and control" (Trujillo 296). Men also have an aura of aggression and violence and they use this aura to obtain sex from women. The language of the body that represents force and competence defines men as "holders of power and in this way, the superiority of men becomes "naturalized" (Connell 92). In this way:

The picture of masculinity has structured by themes of differentiation, separation and independence in contrast with feminine themes of identification, connectedness, and forming relationships and because of this, males are predisposed towards more self-focused and autonomy-driven orientation in society than females. (Thompson 175)

Masculinity as sexual mythology is a set of beliefs and practices that are closely related to sexual differentiation and separation which in Western culture highly relates to patriarchy and patriarchal power. Males are represented as "independent actors such as "breadwinners", "family protectors" and "strong father figures" when women are traditionally seen more as dependent characters such as house wives and sexual objects (Trujillo 305).

When it comes to hegemonic masculinity, in addition to physical force and control, occupational achievement and patriarchy, masculinity also includes the idea of heterosexuality. Traditionally, "men are seen as heterosexual, marital, monogamous, reproductive and non-commercial" (Rubin 296). Some of the main characteristics of masculinity are anti-feminism and heterosexuality. Hegemonic male sexuality includes "certain characteristics which are manifested by adult males through social interaction and relationship with other men and through sexual relationship with women" (Herek 76). Additionally, being a man requires not having sexual relationships with other men and not failing relationships with women.

Although the traditional archetype of masculinity can be seen "as a major part of manhood, some part of masculinity needs to be identified with vanity consumption which is centered on the consumption of beauty and hygiene products, extravagant foods, high culture and high-end couture" (Clarkson 245). For the emerging metro sexual, the search for physical perfection can be seen as a replacing idea for the need of brute force. A metro sexual appearance and a body that does not fit to the traditional myth of masculinity, is challenging the cultural gaze.

The above quotations are ample to show position of women in a patriarchal society. The society, in which V. S. Naipaul was born and brought, has been more or less the same. The overall literary output of Naipaul owes much to the experience of his personal life. People migrating from India in early ages were conservative to their social, religious and cultural conduct. They carry with themselves not only the traditions but the whole nationality where women have specific role within national boundaries. In this chapter we would not only explore but analyze gendered subalternism and the myth of masculinity in Naipaul's *A House for Mr. Biswas, Magic Seeds* and *Half a Life.*

Fragmentation, alienation, and exile are common terms associated with postcolonial literature. Needless to say, imperialism played a key role in bringing a sense of alienation and disorder to the countries where imperialists ruled. One of the best-known writers in English today is

V. S. Naipaul, himself a product of post-imperialist society. To some, he might be better known for the controversial material in his travelogues than for his novels. But this does not undermine his acclaim as a novelist. Naipaul is an expatriate from Trinidad whose primary business as a novelist is to project carefully the complex fate of individuals in a cross-cultural society. He has written extensively about different aspects of post-colonial society, but knowingly or unknowingly, whether he is writing a travelogue or a novel, he tends to end up dealing with the identity crisis of an individual. In an interview with Roland Bryden in 1973, Naipaul remarks:

All my works are really one. I am really writing one big book. I come to the conclusion that, considering the nature of the society I came from, considering the nature of the world I have stepped into and the world I have to look at, I could not be a professional novelist in the old sense. (367-70)

V. S. Naipaul has set these novels in the Indian communities of Trinidad and India. The people living in these communities had firm belief in old tradition as far as women treatment is concerned. The characters Naipaul has produced are archetypes of Indian masses and are highly prejudiced. These women characters are categorized in two major slots- dominating and dominated types although the culture of both is same, with slight difference in their overall condition. They had enough power to maintain the families and control household responsibilities. Despite having so much power, they had to bear reprimand and sometimes severely beaten by their husbands. Discrimination with women is apparent with the fact that these women are from the rich families, yet they are not provided good higher education rather later on confined to their houses.

The women characters of Naipaul are ignorant and innocent. The personal world of women comes to an end with her family. She remains only a component in the household machinery. Her happiness lies in the happiness of the families. Her life is dedicated to the families her happiness shatters if the families suffer. She stays at home minding all their families' responsibilities. Men, on the contrary, remain outside as he has been expected by the society. The statement made by Simon de Beauvoir in her path breaking work *The Second Sex* is quite appropriate to illustrate the role of women in the society:

She is the one who waits, submits, complains, weeps, makes scenes: an ungrateful role that in daily life leads to no apotheosis; as a victim she is looked down on; as a shrew detested; her fate seems the prototype of rapid "recurrence": life only repeats in her, without going anywhere; family set in her role as a housekeeper, she puts a stop to the expansion of existence, she becomes obstacle and negation. (322)

Being a diasporic writer Naipaul writes about the Indian communities especially in Caribbean and Africa where people live with outdated customs and rituals. Female oppression and exploitation, conservative thinking regarding the status of the women in the society and family, dearth of education and obstacle in their progress are the inseparable part of their customs. There are the people like Pt. Ganesh, Mohan Biswas and Willie Chandran who have stepped out of their finite worlds of orthodoxies. They desperately feel the need to change the thinking of the women of their families and want their partner to be equal. Irony lies in the fact that they never made an effort to bring about the change rather they expected the things to happen themselves. These men want educated partner who would understand them and would also accompany them in the course of life.

Naipaul makes it clear that these people want a change but they cannot give up their traditions so easily. Their traditions satisfy their ego and cover most of their shortcomings. The male characters are found laughing at their women's families and ridiculing them intentionally due to their belief in male chauvinism. They derive a sadistic pleasure by tormenting their wives physically and mentally. It allows them to feel happy and content despite being inferior in some respects.

V. Geeta in *Gender* puts gender equal to "caste and religion" as "a part of reality" and thus considers it a vital point of analysis. Gender discrimination is surely an integrated feeling among male dominated societies around the globe. Gender is generally referred to as "a category of analysis" in literary theory. There are various aspects of the societies such as class and caste which "influence" gender in many ways. Therefore, it becomes mandatory to talk about gender in any progressive society to evaluate its depth and type.

A House for Mr. Biswas discusses at length, the ups and downs of Mr. Biswas's life in a typical migrated Hindu community. Mohan Biswas is an exiled Indian "modeled after Naipaul's father" (Ray 19). For Mr. Biswas, life and success means the wonder and audacity of having a house and portion of his own. Naipaul puts forth the struggle of Mr. Biswas in the center of the novel and makes his wife, Shama, an auxiliary to his quest. *A House for Mr. Biswas* is basically a diasporic text where an exiled protagonist tries to establish his identity in an alien world. For him search for a house is the ultimate aim of life. N. Sharda Aiyar in an article *A House for Mr. Biswas: A Study in Cultural Predicament* in the anthology *V. S. Naipaul: Critical Essays* feels, "The sense of being abandoned becomes increasingly acute in the individual as he tries to achieve success and recognition and identity in a pluralistic, post-colonial ruthlessly competitive culture" (Ray 19).

V. S. Naipaul's magnum opus, *A House for Mr. Biswas*, can rightly be called a work of art that deals with the problems of isolation, frustration and negation of an individual. The noveltells the story of its protagonist, Mr. Biswas from birth to death, each section dealing with different phases of his life. Here, Naipaul has a more subjective approach towards the problems of identity crisis than the objective one a reader finds in his travelogues, especially on India.

On the whole the novel is the story of a failed pandit, an accidental journalist and a lost man. In this saga of a man's world women are thrown to the periphery. Women do not stand as the prominent figures, yet they minimally affect the general course of the story. In Mr. Biswas' society women have less space to share. People in such a society believe nature grants superiority to men over women who try to crush them under the patriarchal system. They relegate women to the status of mere "entity" that can be owned or disowned.

Women like Shama and her sisters have seemingly come to a pause regarding their development. They are treated as a piece of property, therefore have become an object of possession. Shama before her marriage is governed by her mother and afterwards by her husband, Mr. Biswas. Naipaul attempts to highlight his qualities for survival in a patriarchal world where indifference to women's sentiments is marked as a sign of manhood.

When we start narrating female character in *A House for Mr. Biswas,* one finds Bipti, Mr. Biswas's mother, a perfect example of stereotypical Indian women. She depends on her husband when she lives with him and on her mother's family when deserted by her husband. A comparison could be drawn between Bipti, as a feeble character and her sister Tara, as an assertive one. But the society does not appreciate Tara for her authoritative nature. Naipaul brings to light the negative attitude of the society towards a powerful woman. Tara is gossiped about when she takes charge of Bipti's family after her husband's death. Bipti, too, willingly gives her children's responsibility to Tara, and sets herself free from the burden of caring. It is evident because Bipti, "who had not been consulted for anything after her husband's death, feels very grateful to Tara and Mr. Biswas gets thrilled at the thought of earning money by being nurtured by his affluent aunt" (*A House for Mr. Biswas* 59).

Bipti is a weak widow and the mother of four sons and a daughter. She has to hide her emotion for her children in front of other due to her dependence on her sister. She could not express her loss when her daughter Dehuti eloped with Tara's low caste yard boy Ramchand. Instead, she shares Tara's outburst for the shame and dishonor her daughter brought to the family. Naipaul shows Bipti lamenting for the loss of her sister's honour not for the loss of her daughter, who was not more than a maid in Tara's house. Dehuti's shameless act is well contrasted with Mr. Biswas' quest for identity as a sign of self-pride. This highlights the difference between the expectation of a society from a boy and a girl child.

"Pastorals," the first section of the novel, describes the birth and early childhood of Mr. Biswas. In this section,

Hindu way of life with its customs, traditions, rituals, and philosophy of the people receives full expression in the small Indian world created by indentured Indian laborers in an artificially created colonial society of Trinidad. But here too, it is the superstitious beliefs, the faith and reliance on pundits which cover the initial pages of the novel. Mr. Biswas has six fingers, a symbol of bad luck for his father and family, and this plays a decisive role in Mohun's life. Mohun is an alien even in his own family as from the very beginning he is declared unlucky in his horoscope. There is something that makes him an outsider in his own Indian world. He becomes a lonely individual who is trying to get a new social role but fails to find it. Naipaul portrays the complexity of the relationship between a man and his origins and his inability to escape from it. Aware of his loneliness and dilemma, Mr. Biswas tells his son, "I am just somebody. Nobody at all" (279). Unlike his father and brothers who have inherited the social identity of labourers, this cannot be claimed by Mr. Biswas.

Mr. Biswas is looking after his uncle's shop while his brothers are working as labourers. After leaving his uncle's store, he takes up a job as sign-painter where he meets Shama, a daughter of the Tulsis (an affluent family of the island), whom he later marries. His marriage makes him realize that life, even after a love-marriage, is not romance, but an act of responsibility. Without money and without a dowry from the Tulsis, Mr. Biswas has no choice but to move in at Hanuman House. He develops a mental complex due to the disagreeable family atmosphere. To Mr. Biswas, it is a typical joint family which functions on the same pattern as the British Empire in West Indies. 'Hanuman House' provides shelter to Mr. Biswas but wants total dilution of his identity in return. In a novel dominated by the house metaphor, Hanuman House is described as follows:

An alien white fortress, the concrete walls looked as thick as they were and when the narrow doors of the Tulsi Store on the ground floor were closed the House became bulky, impregnable and blank. The side walls were windowless and on the upper floors the windows were mere slits in the facade. The balustrade which hedged the flat roof was crowned with a concrete statue of the benevolent Monkey God Hanuman. (*A House for Mr. Biswas* 80-81)

In this way the very structure of Hanuman House makes them subaltern and marginalized as a cocoon of Indian individual indentured laborers.

When Mr. Biswas finds out that men are only needed as husbands and labourers or that they are non-existent in the Tulsi family, his inner self rebels. He finds himself unwanted in Hanuman House which he sees as a communal organization where "he was treated with indifference rather than hostility" (188). Although he tries to win acceptance in the family, he "held his tongue and tried to win favour" (188). This does not mean that he is willing to lose his freedom and independence. When Govind, one of Tulsi son-in-law, suggests that he leaves sign-painting and become a driver for the Tulsi estate, Mr. Biswas immediately voices his dissent: "Give up sign-painting? And my independence? No, boy. My motto is to paddle your own canoe?" (107). It seems that for Mr. Biswas, sign-painting taken up by him voluntarily, has become a part of his identity. He refuses to adopt a profession which is associated with the Tulsis, and he is not ready to merge himself to insignificance like other sons-in-law, some of whose names are even forgotten in the Tulsi family.

To assert his freedom in Hanuman House, Mr. Biswas joins the Aryans, a group of protestant Hindu missionaries from India, and starts advocating the acceptance of conversion and women's education, on the one hand the abolition of the caste system, child marriage, and idol worship, on the other, knowing that these doctrines will anger the Tulsis. Similarly, in order to assert his individuality and to get acknowledged, Mr. Biswas takes up means that are as absurd as they are comic, such as his revenge on Bhandat (spitting in his rum) or giving various nicknames to the Tulsis such as "the old queen," "the old hen," "the old cow" for Mrs.Tulsi, "the big boss" for Seth, the "constipated holy man" and "holy ghost" for Hari, or "the two Gods" for Tulsi's sons. His attitude makes him "troublesome and disloyal and he could not be trusted" (102). Even when Mr. Biswas's daughter is born, it is Seth and Hari who chose the name Savi for his daughter, not Mr. Biswas himself. To register his protest, Mr. Biswas writes on the birth certificate: "Real calling name: Lakshmi. Signed by Mohun Biswas, father. Below that was the date" (163).

Simon De Beauvoir in *The Second Sex* writes about the liberty granted to both sexes:

The mother, as we shall see, is secretly hostile to her daughter's liberation, and she takes to bullying her more or less deliberately: but the boy's effort to become a man is respected, and he is granted much liberty. The girl is required to stay at home, her coming and going are watched; she is in no way encouraged to take charge of her own amusement and pleasure beyond the lack of initiative that is due to women's education, customs make independence different for them. If they roam the streets, they are stared at and accosted. (351-352)

A certain kind of feminism and environmentalism has been utilized in categorical thinking to the advancement of women throughout history. This mode of thinking has worked to keep women away from male because they preserve higher education, intellectual life, art and power. It has effectively confined women to the cramped spaces of the home, to low-paying jobs, denying their mobility, curtailing their desire to go about the world, meet new people and experience life in its magnanimity. Shama in *A House for Mr. Biswas*, Sarojani in *Half a Life* and in *Magic Seeds* are few such examples.

Men have derived a great deal of advantage from "the simple and irrefutable logic of categorization" (Geetha 46). A similar distinction is visible between Mr. Biswas and his sister Dehuti. Mr. Biswas gets an opportunity to go to the school and later on for a training to become a proper "pundit". Whereas, his sister is given to his aunt Tara to learn some "grace" which would help her in getting a match. Bipti is caught thinking:

Bipti had been hoping that Tara would make the suggestion. In four or five years Dehuti would have to be married and it was better that she should be given to Tara. She should learn manners, acquire grace and, with a dowry from Tara, might even make a good match. (*A House for Mr. Biswas* 35)

Shyness and wearing heavy jewellery are a sign of their feminine nature. Dehuti was liked by Tara because she "smiled shyly, not looking up" (35). In Indian society, identity of a girl is always associated with the identity of her husband. His role in her life is that of a "provider." Caste is a matter which is applied to men only; women ethically belong to their provider's caste regardless of their birth in any particular caste. They, as V. Geetha writes, are "feminized in a derogatory sense." The state of women is as demeaning as a "shudra", she argues:

A shudra is like a woman-a case of caste identity being feminized in a derogatory sense. Shudra much like Brahmin and upper caste women, is only fit to serve Brahmin and others, and as with women, in such service lies his salvation. In Hinduism both untouchables and women are polluting — a menstruating woman is literally an untouchable for the days that her period lasts. Gender and class differences are likewise mutually link. (50)

The above statement fits Dehuti's stature suitably. Dehuti by her simple act of eloping with a low caste 'chamar' boy demeans herself completely and she is ousted by her high-caste family. Naipaul presents the attitude of her family post-elopement through Mr. Biswas who visits her place by chance. He feels "that to Dehuti marriage had brought no joy. She was uneasy at being caught among her household possession which was embarrassing for both of them" (71). Dehuti's mental struggle is overpowered by Mr. Biswas's reputation. Her poor and low caste becomes a reason of shame for Mr. Biswas because he is linked with the Tulsis who are well known for their high caste status in Port of Spain. She is not a Brahmin now instead is considered a low caste person. Dehuti in her brother's view is reduced to only without beauty or brains. He could not penetrate her mindset instead he observes her superficially:

Dehuti, never pretty, was now frankly ugly. Her Chinese eyes looked sleepy, the pupils without a light, the whites smudged. Her cheeks, red with pimples, bulged low and drooped around her mouth. Her lower lip projected, as though squashed out by the weight of her cheeks. (*A House for Mr. Biswas* 71)

Naipaul shows Dehuti as an unattractive girl who brings dishonor to her family. He never shows her mental struggle; instead, the repulsion of her brother overpowers the meeting. Dehuti's words and mind do not hold any value for him. It is not so with this demeaned girl only but the rest of the female characters in the text suffer from this servitude and attitude of inferiority. They are conditioned. Shama is taught servitude although she belonged to a rich family and lived in the big house famous as "Hanuman House."

Biswas, being a picaresque figure, goes from pillar to post ascertaining his individual identity, condemns Hanuman House that provides him a false sense of security. No doubt, it provides him bread and butter but at the cost of his individuality. Nevertheless, he successfully overcomes the temptation by flinging all the norms of Tulsis to assert his freedom. This assertion of his authentic self-motivates him to create something out of nothing.

Perpetual humiliation, disgrace and insults aggravate his dilemma. He and his family are subjugated to embarrassment by the people like Seth, Ajodha and Mrs Tulsi. When Anand asks Ajodha, Tara's husband to contribute to a charity fund, he reacts sharply; "You are a funny sort of family. Father collecting money for destitutes. You collecting for Polish refugees. Who collecting for you?" (*A House for Mr. Biswas* 457)

Mr. Biswas's quest led him to the "Honuman House". The next section of the novel "Tulsis" reveals another aspect of Mohun's life. He felt elated and big as "he had been involved in large events and felt that he had achieved a status" (92). He married Shama and started behaving like an adult. Their marriage was like "make-believe" of a child's game. He had "little idea of the problems" that marriage in a patriarchal system would bring to a jobless man. Mr. Biswas already haunted by his nostalgic quest for a home. The question that startled his mind now was:

Where would he live? What would happen to his mother? His condition was pathetic because he had no money and job, for sign-writing, while good enough for a boy living with his mother, was hardly a secure profession for a married man. (95)

Hanuman House is governed by Mrs. Tulsi, commonly known as the big boss. Naipaul shows a dichotomy by contrasting Mr. Biswas's thinking and other sons-in law of the family, who unobjectionably accept the supremacy of Mrs. Tulsi. Naipaul shows Shama's house as an overcrowded monkey house where a mother with all the daughters and son-in law, and her sister and brother-in law live. In such a house where matriarchy seems to prevail overtly, Mr. Biswas fears his identity and faces a hard time to save his manhood despite being a declared failure. His philosophy of paddle your own canoe gets wounded when his career as a sign painter could not provide him with bread and butter. If the text is diasporic in nature on the one hand, then on the other it also brings forth psychological complexities produced by the clash between matriarchy and patriarchy.

Naipaul presents Shama as a properly trained woman by the patriarchy. She displays her discomfiture for Mr. Biswas's status as a dependent of Tulsis. She considers herself inferior to her brothers and sisters due to her husband's incompetence to provide them bread and butter. Her other brothers-in law is not independent, so they cooperate with Mr. Tulsi and contribute in family income. On the contrary, Mr. Biswas considered it below his dignity to give help to her family. He considered it as the trick of Tulsis for they strangled and exploited everyone. He observed and comments that sisters "had, in the Tulsi marriage lottery, drawn husbands with money and position; these daughters followed the Hindu custom of living with their husbands's family, and formed no part of the Tulsi organization" (*A House for Mr. Biswas* 97).

In this way we find that Naipaul is capturing the attention of the characters searching for a permanent foothold. The novel depicts houses as the predominant metaphor signifying the universal diasporic disorder. The hero of the novel Mohun Biswas represents the psychology of every East–Indian colonial at Trinidad. He endeavors to create something significant and substantial out of the unimportant, uncreative, cynical Trinidad" (124).

Biswas is a more complex version of Ganesh as he also follows the same process of growing up from nothing. His sense of alienation and homelessness is perhaps derived from the character of *Miguel Street*. His life is a complex tale of an expatriate Indian's ambivalence presenting the typical expatriate sensibility. Mr. Biswas, whose life-long ambition is the ownership of a house, finds him caught in an inescapable trap. Thus, the symbol of house embodies Naipaul's personal diasporic predicament.

Biswas's individual quest for selfhood, identity and coherence in his life terminates with the ownership of a house of his own. Though the multiple defects and drawbacks of the house lessen his charm still he is excited because he has now found some meaning in his existence in the world. He exclaims, "How terrible it would have been to have lived and died as one had been born, unnecessary and un-accommodated" (54).

The darkness, decay, death, horror and disasters recurrent in Biswas's life represent his nothingness and also the nothingness of his surroundings. In the epilogue, Naipaul shows the depth of this inherent darkness, "This was a darkness that seemed to come from within, as though the skin was murky but transparent film and the flesh below it had been bruised and become diseased and its corrupting was rising" (*A House for Mr. Biswas* 587-88).

Mohun Biswas's continual acceptance and condemnation in his own family, in Tulsi family, Sentinel Office, Community Welfare Department and in Trinidadian society as a whole mark the typical dilemma of an un-housed and uprooted expatriate. His constant encounter with oddity, adversity and misfortune makes his life unbearable. Certain economic changes, global wars, introduction to cinema and motor cars, brain-drain and arrival of Americans in bulk, ect. have made an impact on the social scenario of Trinidad considerably. Naipaul's obsession however, as N. Ramadevi observes, primarily intends to unfold:

The gradual Indian accommodation to what was originally a foreign land. The process involves a great deal of sacrifice--- a sacrificing of traditions and self-respect leading to an acculturisation and mimicry. First of all, the people have to be dispossessed of what is naturally and originally there . . .. A gradual decay of Hindu spirit in the New World which could be evidence in the marriages of the Tulsi sons to Presbyterian Indians. (54)

The plight of immigrant-indentured laborers from India is the pivot of the novel suggesting their unavoidable helplessness and alienation as they are left with no other option but to curse their destiny. The first generation of indentured laborers at Parrot Trace seems to have established a community life that is in no way different from an Indian village. Naipaul vividly describes the agony of such unwelcomed expatriates missing their past and native culture but now they feel entrapped and experience a common loss. The old Indian-born homesick people gather in the arcade of Tulsi in the evening only to talk about their retreat to their homeland.

Women in Naipaul's novels are rarely appealing. Shama by her looks charmed Biswas in the first glance but her childish behavior was enough to make his "disenchantment complete". Leela in *Mystic Masseur* appeals Pt. Ganesh initially when he saw her peeping from behind the curtain. Willie's mother in *Half a Life* was a medium of sacrifice for Chandran; an excuse to live according to Gandhi's ideology. They commonly lack sense of aesthetics. They are either frankly ugly or tolerably common. They are never attributed exceptional traits so that they could attract men permanently towards them. It is a man's world where women have a very little importance. Mr. Biswas is a powerful only for Shama otherwise he is a failure. He is beaten by everyone in the Hanuman house due to his ill behavior and bad temper. His shame and defeat is exerted in the form of his frustration and anguish on Shama. His masochistic obsession over her is a camouflage for his inferiority and failure.

Mr. Biswas's "underemployment" and low earning dwarfs Shama in front of her relatives. Shama suffered a loss, which is felt equally by her husband. Their marriage brought "sadness and deep sense of loss" (*A House for Mr. Biswas* 99). Both of them feel lonely. Mr. Biswas refuses to be commanded by anyone rather he wants its reverse. So, he discovers the way to impose his supremacy over his wife and her relatives. His sarcasm is one of his tricks he applies on Shama. He calls Shama's brothers "the little gods" as they are given a separate luxurious room in Hanuman

House on their return from their education. Mr. Biswas could not bear this and starts behaving weirdly with everyone in the house including his own wife.

Both of Shama's brothers are sent to school for better education. The elder "attended the Roman Catholic college" and the "younger was being coached to enter the college." There was no provision for the girls in the family to visit college for further education. Marriage was thought fit for their future. To be born as a boy in an Indian family meant in Trinidad to belong to a privileged category naturally. In Tulsi family girl education is looked down upon. Mrs. Tulsi's remark reflects her attitude, "So you want girl children learning to read and write and picking up boy-friends? You want to them wearing frocks?" (*A House for Mr. Biswas* 124)

Boys are fed on good food because they are superior lot in the family. V. Geetha puts forth further distinction, "Girls in poor families get to eat less food than boys. They are less likely to be sent to school, less favoured when it comes to buying new clothes or toys" (31-32). This trend is continued through generations. It was among Shama and her brothers, Mr. Biswas and his sister, Savi and Anand and so on. With their growing age the children in such families understand their roles. V. Geetha says, "Many things seem to suggest that it is natural and inevitable for men and women to pursue different paths and seek particular and exclusive destinies" (32). Shama unintentionally expects Mohun to bring the things and feed the family. It is Mohun's socially expected role that he would never try to understand his wife instead he would relate her with inferior qualities. He comments and satirizes her family on every occasion without fail.

Naipaul's men like Mohun, Ganesh and Willie Chandran think that women are no match to their intelligence. They are inferior by birth. This imposed inferiority gives way to men to ridicule their sentiments. Mohun does so by intention to Shama and she either has to keep silent or will receive physical torture. Here Naipaul portrays Mohun teasing Shama by ridiculing her relatives:

'How the little gods getting on today, eh?

He would ask.

He meant her brothers .....

'How the hods, eh?

Shama wouldn't reply.

'And how the Big Boss getting on today?' that was Seth......

And how the old queen?' that was Mrs. Tulsi.

'The old hen? The old cow?'

'Family? Family? This blasted fowl run you calling family? (*A House for Mr. Biswas* 104-05)

Shama accepts her lot as a passive listener but when Mr. Biswas becomes intolerable, she has to retaliate. His ego is hurt by Shama' words, "you can't give me anything consequently he temporarily abandons Hanuman House" (107). As Naipaul portrays women, they always create turbulent dramatic scenes like Shama, Chinta and Padma to draw attention. This is a characteristic which is typically associated with the powerless species that use it as their weapon against oppression. They make issues out of non-issue. Mr. Biswas soothes and nourishes his pride by abusing Shama's family as "a fowl run" or "monkey house" or a "blasted zoo" or a "low caste bunch" (120). More than Shama, Mr. Biswas created nuisance in Hanuman House for which they had to leave for "Chase", a nearby town in Port of Spain. In Chase a closed house and shop awaited their arrival with "the smell of grease". Shama indignantly held her husband responsible for their banishment. She disliked every action of Mr. Biswas and he never confined in her. She felt martyred at her husband's indecent behavior and the distance between them always haunted their relationship. Mr. Biswas always underestimated her emotions and Shama thought him "stupid, boring and shaming" (*A House for Mr. Biswas* 143).

As a contrast to Mr. Biswas, Shama is a dull girl; even then she seems to adjust better than him in adverse condition. It was Shama who "produced a meal" (146) in that garbage house in Chase and told him how to run a shop while Mr. Biswas was still fumbling. Naipaul writes:

He knew nothing about keeping books and it was Shama who had suggested that he should make notes of good given on credit on squares of brown shop papers. It was Shama who suggested that these squares should be spiked . . .. It was Shama who made the accounts. (147)

Naipaul's description of Shama carries the features of a typical Indian girl who handles the things with great subtlety along with the nagging habits. Mr. Biswas was amazed to see Shama nag for the first time in his life, "It has puzzled him. Living in wife-beating society, he couldn't understand why women were even allowed to nag or how nagging could have any effect" (148).

Naipaul dissects the Hindu society and examines the roles of men and women in Indian society. He categorizes women in two groups—first those who nag and are dominated and the other who dominate. He saw that "there are exceptional women, Mrs. Tulsi and Tara, for example who could never be beaten" (148). On the other hand, wives take their husband's habit of beating as a matter of "pride". Sushila, Shams's widowed sister "regarded them as a necessary part of her training and often attributed the decay of Hindu society in Trinidad to the rise of timorous, weak, non-beating class of husbands" (148).

Shusila and Leela in *The Mystic Masseur* are a case in point. The society has assigned for them befitting their gender. In India, women as a wife are expected to be "patient, understanding, emotionally expressive and compassionate" (Geetha 35). The women in Hanuman House and in all these texts efficiently adopt their pre-assigned roles. They conceive their passive roles as the sign of dignity. Being a man "means that one is rational, always in control, unemotional and consistently strong" (Geetha 35). Mr. Biswas falling short of manly qualities in a predefined society "cultivates a huge sense of inferiority for not being man enough" (36).

Mr. Biswas' quest for identity and for a house of his own is a manifestation of his desire to be known as a "complete man." He knows that the definition of "man" compulsorily involves the ability to be the "owner" with authority. Biswas craved throughout his life for a permanent shelter in order to satisfy his ego; "occupy positions of power, prestige and authority" (36). His desire to control was unfulfilled at Hanuman House. He behaved, remarkably in an uncivilized, quarrelsome way to Tulsis because they overpowered him and tried to crush him.

The women in Mr. Biswas's life are his mother, aunt, wife and his daughter Savi, Myna and Kamla. Mr. Biswas in any case did not want Savi to learn Hanuman House etiquettes. Savi was perfect like any Indian girl as she was "dispirited and submissive" and "afraid" of her father (222). Any resemblance of her daughter with his wife was tormenting for him. He felt Savi looked like Shama he felt "that Savi had betrayed him" (*A House for Mr. Biswas* 223).

Mr. Biswas has moved away and yet he feels trapped in Hanuman House. He had three children and his wife is pregnant with the fourth. He is terrified of future. The only thing that "gave him comfort" was that "he had claimed Savi" (227). Savi as a daughter is a source of comfort because she satisfies her father's male ego by listening quietly him. She does not argue with him like Shama.

Children are given toys according to their gender. It prepares them for their roles in the society in future. Mr. Biswas gifts a "doll house" to Savi, but a toy car to his son Anand. In Savi, thus, her girlhood is involved by her parents and the people around her, which is a common thing in any conventional society. V. Geetha writes, "Parents dress their boy and girl children in different ways. They buy them different toys and books" (31). It was expected from Savi to cry when "doll house" was broken by Shama whereas Anand's timidity is hated by her father as boys must not cry.

In utter frustration, Mr. Biswas behaves savagely towards Shama to the extent of kicking her "on her belly" during her fourth pregnancy. Despite her will to rebel, Shama can never refute rather continues to live in suffocation. Contrary to this he enjoyed her discomfiture and used it very often by offending her. When Mr. Biswas had made his wooden house ready, Shama went to live in it. He feels depressed when Shama comes to stay with him because he suffers from an inferiority complex. He thinks that Shama would ridicule his incapability in the absence of the other members of her family. In its furious reaction he tries to kill himself along with his two elder children but he didn't want to kill Myna and Shama as he "didn't care" for them. He tries to show his indifference for Shama, because Shama's sheer presence irritates him. "He was violently angry; never before disgusted by her" (275). He was drawn to such a disgusting idea like suicide as a consequence of his incompetent manhood. She continuously reminds him of his failure as a husband and father both.

Mr. Biswas and people like him never appreciate their wives for their help during their struggle. The illiteracy and stereotypical behavior of women aroused repulsion in these men. Mr. Biswas is seen praising the beauty of the co-workers in the "Sentinel" office several times. His attempts to write a story often revealed his desire to "possess" women who behaves in a very sophisticated manner. Mr. Biswas finally manages to own a house of his own after multiple failures. He calls this house the "perfect" house. He dies in that house leaving behind his wife and three daughters, where as his son is sent abroad for further studies. All his daughters despite their sharp intellect are left with nothing in their lives. Their father never thought of sending them abroad for further studies. They follow the same life pattern which their mother and aunts as their "natural" way of life. They end up becoming like their mother and the rest of the women in the family.

Most of these girls have never been to the boundary of the college. They were confined to the four walls of their house. Their knowledge is limited to writing and reading letters in a funny way, be that Shama or Leela or Sarojini. There is a wide difference in the level of education of Willie and Sarojini, Leela and Ganesh, and Mr. Biswas and Shama.

Naipaul presents the customs of Hindu society and character's inclination towards these customs. Hanuman House stands out as an exception because it had a very "untraditional organization where married daughters lived with their mother" (*A House for Mr. Biswas* 365). In such a society it is expected that mothers-in-law would be "hard on daughters-in-law" and "sisters-in-law would be despised." Whenever any other female from an alien society enters such a household, she is taken aback by the surprising attitudes. They are criticized by other family members for refusing to conform to their conventional ways.

Women in Indian society hardly take initiative in sexual matters and often condemn women of "other race" for their "sexual appetite." Padama condemns Dorothy for her allegedly insatiable desires. Indian women feel hesitant in other matters. Shama finds it difficult to talk to the "women of other race" as she was "shy of people of another race, religion or way of life" (366).

In *A House for Mr. Biswas* women are often left alone in their limited worlds and are never considered as companions by their men. Shama too is left alone with her tenants in Hanuman House while Mohun and his children go to visit Ajodha and Tare every weekend. Shama feels the "need of company" due to her loneliness. It is not so that his absence gives her a sense of loneliness rather she feels more alone in his presence because of Mr. Biswas's regular habit of quarreling with her and her family members. His tendency to fight with everyone leads to his boycott from her sisters and other relatives. Here too, Shama is the sufferer due to her gender as she cannot initiate any communication, whereas Mr. Biswas can do it only by virtue of being a male.

Naipaul shows a wide difference between the status of women in Indian society and other communities. Comparing the women of *A House of Mr. Biswas* and of *Half a Life*, there is a huge difference between the two. Shama, a conservative uneducated stereotype girl is a hurdle in Mr. Biswas's progress. Whereas Willie's mother and his wife Ana in *Half a Life* are graduates and understand their men to a certain limit, yet they are considered as obstacles. Willie's mother always falls short of his father's expectations. She is a "backward caste" girl whom Chandran never married. Therefore, she could not achieve a respectable place in India where marriage is looked at as an important institution. Chandran could never share his emotions with his wife as he never felt associated with her. Chandran was under great influence of Mahatma Gandhi when he saw her in his college. Gandhi called the youth of India to defy the caste system by inter-caste marriages. He thought to live a "life of sacrifice and this girl became the victim of his infirm decision" *(Half a Life* 12). Naipaul writes in the novel about this girl without name from Chandran's point of view:

There was a girl at the university. I didn't know her. I hadn't spoken to her. I had merely noticed her. She was small and coarse-featured, almost tribal in appearance, noticeable black, with two big top teeth that showed very white. She wore colors that were sometime very bright and sometime very muddy, seeming to run into the blackness of her skin. She would belong to a backward cast. (*Half a Life* 11)

Chandran without taking her emotions into consideration proposed her in a very timid manner. She becomes a victim of hatred unintentionally. Naipaul writes that Chandran felt "repelled, ashamed, moved" and instead of love "there came a little sympathy" (12) in his heart for her. She is victimized due to her low caste status and gender. She is a either speechless or stunned by his sinister decision about family matters and her own children.

The idea of sacrifice is imposed on her by Chandran. She never invited him for the marriage of this sort. She was made to live with him due to his whim to follow "Gandhi's call" to marry low caste girls and boys so as to blur the caste distinctions. She suffers Chandrna's decision throughout because Chandran was never firm on his decisions and repents later on. But there is no excuse now for him as he has already started living with her. She is often accused and abused by Chandran for her low caste manners, because for him she is "uneducated inherently". She is shown as a rough and insensitive woman as the mark of her low caste status. Chandran should have thought it before marrying her. He is a feeble character who never had the courage to face his mistakes.

Naipaul narrates the story from Chandran's point of view; therefore, he becomes an object of subordination. Chandran's making all the important decisions of his family without her consent leads to family feuds. She is not an exceptional case, but almost all the women in Naipaul's texts are unable to carve an important place in their family. They are all timid and abide by the patriarchal law, their status as a housewife makes them indifferent to the world and its various other dimensions.

As it is visible in each and every society that men are privileged by patriarchal law and expect an unconditional servitude. As J. S. Mill observed in 19th century in his *On the Subjection of Women* that "all men, expect the most brutish, desire to have, in the women most nearly connected with them, not a forced slave but a willing one, not a slave merely, but a favorite" (14).

She serves Chandran throughout her life willingly, yet she is not given a proper place in his life. She loves her son Willie beyond the fact that he was entirely different from her and never associated with her. In these texts it is distinctly visible that a "woman" feels satisfied and considers her life meaningful if she can assist him in "his individualistic pursuit. She has other independent existence. She has no individual identity. She ultimately will have to return to her man at the end so does Shama. She gives herself physically, emotionally and mentally to her husband by making "him" her; but in return she has no right to expect security. "Love" as a feeling is a far-fetched idea for these women.

Willie is the only hope to his mother, yet he deserts her like his father. He always had negative thoughts for his mother even during his college time in England. He associates her with everything ugly; his friend Percy's bad taste of colours reminds him of his mother's colour choice. Willie thinks, "A fussiness about cloth and colour was something he associated with women and in a now secret part of his mind he thought of the backwards on his mother's side, and their love of strong colour" (*Half a Life* 64).

All these men desert their wives at a certain point of time, some literally and some stop talking to them. As Willie used Ana and then deserts her just because he was "fed up living her life." He gave words to his desire of living alone while taking the best of her life as he narrates to his sister that when she came back later, I said to her, "I am forty-one. I am tired of living your life" (Half *a Life* 227). Willie shows his selfishness by ignoring Ana's point of view. He acknowledged her services and, felt the gratitude for her as he confessed to her at the time of departure:

I know, you did everything for me. You made it easy for me here. I couldn't have lived here without you. When I asked you in London I was frightened? I had nowhere to go. They were going to throw me out of the college at the end of the term and I didn't know what I could do keep afloat. (*Half a Life 227)*

Willie, like every protagonist of Naipaul, picks up the job of writing in the newspapers and contributes to BBC news with "awkward stories" of his childhood. He was an out and out failure. With the help of Ana he could achieve the confidence to live on his own. In case of Ana, the relationship is different, as Willie is financially and prestigiously dependent on her. In spite of her dominating status, she never overpowered him. It was Willie who took pleasure and profit from her stature. The women maintain the serenity and peace in their matrimony by their ability to tolerate and ignore the sneer of their men.

In a few cases women's agony becomes acute by the virtue of their individual weakness. Shama is the case in point. She suffers doubly; firstly, through her husband, and secondly by her family's consequential response. Leela, too, has to bear the torture of her husband due to her childlessness. She suffers both as an abandoned mother and wife. Ana suffered Willie's selfishness post-marriage. Ana, in spite of belonging to non-Indian community, has to accept Willie's treachery and deception. She witnessed Willie's and Graca's increasing incestuous relations, without a sign of agitation on her face she bore all the insult including Willie's confesses to Ana: "We made live in the house, Graca and I, as it was being built" (219). Despite the despotic nature of their husbands, they do not revolt against them as they continue to live with them. They adopt a submissive role on the domestic front. Mostly they surrender to the will of their men and follow the norms laid by the society.

Willie's sister Sarojini is seen in the image of his mother as he calls her the "little ugly Sarojini." Her father never wished to send her to abroad or college for higher education. Due to her marriage she manages to visit England once and her brother too in his hostel. He feels "repelled" by the "smell of the food she prepared in the little hostel room." Sarojini stands as a symbol of Chandran's failure and thus poses a threat to his reputation. Consequently, Willie feels ashamed of her presence in his hostel room in England. He disliked her Indian way of dressing. He avoids introducing her to his college friends.

Sarojini is not sent abroad for higher education like her brother. For her father Sarojini is a constant cause of worry. The only better prospects he could devise for her is an "international marriage". He finds a lame German war photographer who was already married with two children. It is important to note that girls are seen as a burden and are dispensed with no sense of regret. She is somehow married and is left to her destiny. This German photographer deserts Sarojini in Germany and has no feelings for her. She was treated as subaltern.

After leaving Ana, Willie seeks support from his sister. She is comfortable even in adverse situation. She had no complications, no fabricated lies, and no unreal conceptions to lead in her problems like her brother Willie. She adjusts naturally and never feels awkward due to her Indian identity. She provides support to her brother in his dire need. On the contrary he still feels the same repulsion for the "food that Sarojini cooked in the small stale-smelling kitchen at the back" (*Half a Life* 137). Willie observes a change in her dressing sense as "She had given up the style of sari and cardigan and socks. She was in jeans and a heavy sweater and her manner was brisker and even more authoritative than Willie remembered" (Half *a Life* 137-138).

Willie abhors his poor adjustability in awkward situations when he sees Sarojini living a comfortable life. He is compelled to think that all her oddity was buried in the girl now, whom he had left behind him at home. She had come a long way as she seems "attractive." Willie also guesses about her being in love with otherwise he would have probably been lost in nothingness if the women in his life, like Ana, June, and Sarojini would not have supported him. He narrates the role of Ana in his life to Sarojini:

I drew comfort from Ana, her strength and authority. And just as now, as you may have noticed, Sarojini, I lean on you, so in those days, ever since she had agreed to my being with her in Africa, I leaned on Ana. I believed in a special way in her luck, some of this had to do with the very fact that she was a woman who had given herself to me. (*Half a Life* 141)

Willie had always been "protected" and "guided" by one or the other women in some essential way. In his childhood it was his mother, in youth June and Ana, and in his later life it is his sister who cares for him. He completely depends on Ana during his stay in Portuguese Africa in her grandfather's house. Naipaul thus comments through him that in Indian culture "men are really looking for women to lean on" (141). Naipaul here draws a difference between two women from different communities. Both of them have different ideas, Sarojini follows her "firebrand" maternal uncle's radical genes and is furious in nature; whereas Ana is different in her thinking due to her racial and social difference. Willie cherished this difference in Ana and despised Sarojini. Ana was "important" for him because he depended on her for his idea of being a man in his beginning years but Sarojini becomes the need for his survival in his later life.

In medieval India "sati system" was followed with a pure religious dedication. The society had no guilt in burning the widowed wife on her husband's pyre. Bipti, Mr. Biswas's mother who is born in modern times is not burned but she has to suffer the painful phase of widowhood. She leads the life of alienation and seclusion devoid of all the pleasures after the death of her considerably incompetent husband. Now she was to be avoided in all pious ceremonies of her family and could not perform any ritual as she is seen as the inauspicious sight in her very house. Naipaul narrates that touchy moment of proclamation of her widowhood in a series of prolonged rituals which is enough to give an idea of patriarchy prevalent in these societies:

Bipti was bathed. Her hair, still wet, was neatly parted and the parting filled with red henna. Then henna was scooped out and the paring filled with charcoal dust. She was now a widow forever. Tara gave a short scream and at the signal the other women began to wail. (*A House for Mr. Biswas* 32)

This episode is marked with irony and sarcasm as these customs are over and no more followed in modern times yet it remains effective among conventional people. They follow that age old system which takes pride in making a widow's life hell without feeling ashamed of its oddity. Bipti, Sarojini and Shama remain submissive throughout the novels and they could not get recognition by their husbands. In the society like that the future of girls are decided by their parents. They are very rarely given the opportunity to develop. On the other hand, boys are granted more liberty and enjoy the freedom of making their own choices. Sarojini in *Half a Life* is brought up with same ideology. A letter to Willie from his father reveals his biased attitude:

I write now with news of your sister Sarojini . . .. Well, a German came one day. He was an oldish man with a bad leg. Well, to cut a long short, he asked to marry Sarojini, and that is what precisely he had done. You will know that I always felt that Sarojini's only hope lay on an international marriage, but I must say this took me surprise. I am sure he has a wife somewhere, but perhaps isn't good to ask too much. (*Half a Life* 112)

Chandran is worried for his daughter's marriage to the extent that he closes his eyes to the general good of her. Thus, he does not hesitate to wed her to an undeserving man without seeking her consent. As Naipaul shows in the above incident that girls cannot have their choice in the most private decisions like their own wedding. This instance is not only painful but also highly condemnable that a father may overlook his daughter's emotions and defy the bond of affection. They have to compromise at each and every step due to this mindset. They lack efficiency to stand on their own; therefore, they cannot rebel. They have to bear the suppression of their husbands, who compel them to adopt the passive roles. Their condition is worse than the bonded slave as they can't voice their views and are silenced most of the times. The men in the family limit their needs to clothing and food. They forget their emotional aspect very comfortably. She is a "doll" to be decorated and showcased; a plaything and an object of possession. She has to dress up the way men like them to dress. Simon de Beauvoir gives way to her angst on this issue in *The Second* Sex:

Paralyzed by inconvenient clothing and by the same rules of propriety--- then women's body seems to men to be his property, his thing. Make-up and jewelry also further this petrifaction of face and body. The function of ornamental attire is very complex; with certain primitives it has a religious significance: but more often its purpose is to accomplish the metamorphosis of women into idol. (167)

Works Cited

Bama. *Kurukku*. Translated by Lakshmi Holmstrom. Chennai: McMillion, 2000. Print.

Beauvoir, Simon De. "The Mother." *French Feminism Reader*. Ed. Kelly Oliver. Lanham: Rowaman, 2000. Print.

Clarkson, J. "Contesting Masculinity's Makeover: Queer Eye, Consumer Masculinity,

and Straight Acting Gays." *Journal of Communication Inquiry* 29.3 (2005): 235-255.

Connell, R. W. "An Iron Man: The Body and Some Contradictions of Hegemonic

Masculinity." *Sport, Men and the Gender Order: Critical Feminist Perspectives*. Eds. M. A. Meissner and D. F. Sabo. Champaign: Human Kinetics, 1990. 83-95.

Geetha, V. *Gender: Theorizing Feminism*. New Delhi: Street, 2001. Print.

Greenhalgh, Susan. *Madoc-Jones*. London: OUP, 1966. Print.

Hanke, R. "Hegemonic Masculinity in Something." *Critical Studies in Mass*

Communication 7.3 (1990): 231-248. Print.

Herek, G. M. "On Heterosexual Masculinity: Some Psychical Consequences of the

Social Construction of Gender and Sexuality." *Changing Men: New Direction in Research on Men and Masculinity*. Ed. M. S. Kimmel.Newbury Park: Sage, 1987. Print.

Naipaul, V. S. "Writer Without Roots." *The New York Times Magazines*. Dec 26,

1976. 19-22. Print.

---. *A House for Mr. Biswas.* London: Andre Deutsch, 1961. Print.

---. *Half a Life*. London: Picador, 2001. Print.

Nayar, Pramod K. *Postcolonial Literature: An Introduction*. New Delhi: Pearson,

2008. Print.

Pronger, B. *The Arena of Masculinity: Sports, Homosexuality, and the Meaning of*

Sex. New York: St. Martin's Press. 1990. Print.

Rubin, G. "Thinking Sex: Notes for a radical theory of the politics of sexuality."

Pleasure and danger: Exploring Female Sexuality. Ed. C. Vance.Boston: Routledge, 1985. 267-319. Print.

Thompson, C. J. "Marketplace Mythology and Discourses of Power." *Journal of*

Consumer Research 31.1 (2004): 162-180. Print.

Trujillo, N. "Hegemonic Masculinity on the Mound: Media Representations of Nolan

Ryan and American Sports Culture." *Critical Studies in Mass Communication* 8.3 (1991): 290-308. Print.

Wirsching, M. "Race to the Top: Masculinity, Sport, and Nature. "*Men and Masculinity* 10.2

(2007): 197-221. Print.

CHAPTER TWO

Subaltern Voices in An Area of Darkness, India: A Wounded Civilization and India: A Million Mutinies Now

When a group is socially marginalized in comparison to the majority host culture, it is called 'minority group'. The term 'ethnic' has been placed as a prefix before the name of community such as, ethnic Indian, ethnic Turks and so on. In literature ethnicity works as an identity phenomenon meaning the search for self. It defines the social boundary of the ethnic group and develops a strategy of acquiring the resources one needs to survive. The diasporic force which emerges from identity formation becomes ethnicity. The Indian community has become an ethnic group, sharing cultural values, languages, territorial contiguity and is distinguishable from the other group.

Ethnicity is a new experience for a long suppressed or undermined and disadvantaged person who was now seeking political "redress in society" (Bell 169). Ethnicity removed their bitter experience of a "suspended identity" Which was the result of the Indian community being treated like a marginal group.

The term 'ethnicity' appeared for the first time in 1972 in a supplement of *The Oxford Dictionary*. It is used to analyze the socio-political demands. Its meaning was an ethnic pride of the group, having a common belonging,sharing socio-cultural norms and ethics. "Ethnicity being a functional process, it provides a social bond where inscriptive structures have been eroded, it is less divisive than integrating in many cases, it facilitates a common language" (Allardt 18). Ethnicity functions as an identity phenomenon, meaning a search for self. It defines the social boundary of the ethnic group and develops a strategy of achieving the resources one requires to survive. The process of its velocity becomes a forceful power of Ethnicity. Ethnicity as mentioned in the *Intercocta-Glossary*is "Involving an inscriptive, genetically self-perpetuating mode of social relations treated as an alternative to, or complement of, other forms of social organization, in the context of a larger society" (Riggs 4).

Ethnicity is an important characteristic of human identity and it manifests differently in different societies. It reflects diversity in the society whose internal harmony and stability defends on how ethnic diversity is accommodated in a pluralistic frame work of the state and society. In developing world ethnic politics is one of the reasons of internal instability in the society. Ethnic conflicts lead towards ethnic politics which is often conceived as a conflict among ethnic groups.

The study of the politics of ethnicity highlights various problems of diasporic people in all over the world when they confront different cultures. At that time ethnicity becomes an important concern as one shift one's location and becomes a member of minority community in an alien environment. A shift in locational status makes one conscious of their ethnic identity.

Ethnicity is used with the help of political participation to obtain resources and recognition from the host societies. Kipling expresses these sentiments in following lines:

"The Stranger within my gate, He may be true or kind
But he does not talk my talk. I cannot feel his mind
I see the face and the eyes and the mouth, But not the soul behind
The men of my own stock they may do ill or well,
But they tell me lies I wanted to; they are used to the lies I tell;
And we do not need interpreters when we go to buy or sell." (*Best of Attack and National Vangard* 65)

V.S. Naipaul once, or often, described his purpose as an author as nothing less than a commitment to deliver the truth. Now what is truth in one particular span of time, in one particular sphere and to a particular community or part of world and to a subsequent generation? This alteration doesn't transform the former truth in untruth but in half-truth or tangential truth. Since the former truth fails in retaining its complete veracity and genuineness, writers established truth but they should be revealing the newly emerged peculiarity and discovering the new vicissitudes.

The world being mobile and not static is assuming each new day a new facet and negating its yester. So, this world is always new and infinite. This newness and infinity are always a favorite theme among writers so with Naipaul also. Mel Gussow writes:

How much the modern world does his work contain? You should be able to see the lineaments of today's society in the work of a good writer. I just feel that we are living in such an interesting world. One must capture all the interest of this period. I don't believe that the entire world has all been written about. The world is so new. (Gussow 19)

This realization came to Naipaul only in 70s and *An Area of Darkness* subtitled as 'Experience of India' had already been published in 1962. This book is the first of his reputed trilogy on India and charts out writers first hand impression about India in which he talks about Indian traditions and her mythical importance.

Ethnic identity or diasporic identity relies on ancestral ties, kinship relations, common language of communication, historical and imaginary memories and religious beliefs, it became a shield to protect, preserve and maintain the ethnic culture. Ethnicity took this baggage and exposed it to the host culture. V. S. Naipaul first visited India in 1962 to locate his roots in a distant village of Eastern Uttar Pradesh. His search for identity in an "imaginary homeland" made him discover whole India. He felt nostalgic about the image of his homeland carved on his mindset by the descriptions of his forefathers. His first visit, however, could not bring him close to India; Instead, it made him "hysterical" he got disillusionment with its much talked about glory. Naipaul visited India several times to understand nature of his relationship with it. Naipaul explores a cultural paradox in a country widely known for its cultural heritage, which he expresses in his famous trilogy.

Naipaul finds the present India all confusing and an indistinguishable amalgam of various races, cultures, faiths and beliefs. It is his minute observation and sharp analysis of Indian plight of political stumble and economic failure. He says India like Vijaynagar has not been able to divorce its past. India, according to him is nothing more than the ruins poled up. It lives in the "fantasy of past splendor". Naipaul catches up the dichotomy between the past and the present while looking at the temple of Vijaynagar as he writes:

To the pilgrim, Vijayanagar is its surviving temple. The surrounding destruction is like proof of the virtue old magic; just as the fantasy of the past splendor is accommodated within as acceptance present squalor. That glorious avenue is a slum. Life goes on, the past continues. After conquest and destruction, the past simply reassert itself. (*India: A Wounded Civilization* 5)

Civilization of any country consists not only of men and women but of their beliefs, customs, assumption, living style, manners and achievements in literature, science, art, polity and economic development etc. For our better understanding we may mention Edward Burnett:

Culture or civilization, taken in its widest ethnographic sense is that complex while which includes knowledge, belief, art, morals, law, customs and any other capabilities and habits acquired by man as a member of society. (Burnet

7)

Naipaul understands his limitation due to his relationship with India. His India lineage is not sufficient for him to be known as Indian; instead, it further intensifies his uneasiness. He cannot remain indifferent to Indian as he remains in case of Egypt or Middle East. India of Naipaul's dream had been superseded by an India teeming with children, the dirt, the disease, the undernourishment, the cries of baksheesh, the hawkers and the touts, etc.

*An Area of Darkness*is rationally the most emotional and individual book of the trilogy. It describes Naipaul's first trip to the country of his forefathers, which was evidently a very emotive experience for the author, and therefore, the writer could not remain unmoved. The novel is not a mere objective description typical of travel books, but it shows the reader a picture of India seen through the eyes of one of the most excellent observers, who has a very intimate relationship with the country through his ancestors. Naipaul does not hesitate to reveal his true feelings about India and gives the reader very melancholic and ironical depictions of what he observes.

He came to India to locate his roots with certain preconceived notions which had been shaped in his psyche since his boyhood. Naipaul explores the reasons for its "present squalor" by tracing India's historic upheavals. His interest in this inquiry is due to his strange relationship with India. India for him cannot be any other "common country" offering him only "beautiful sights". He says:

And India had in a special way been the background of my childhood. It was the country from which my grandfather came, a country never physically described and therefore never real, a country out in the void beyond the dot of Trinidad. It was a country suspended in time; it couldn't be related to the country discovered later. (*An Area of Darkness* 39-40)

Naipaul also makes a fun of Indians saying that they imitate the English. They have borrowed their language, traditions and customs, although it does not really make sense to Indians. They do not care about a deeper meaning of these practices. The Indian command of English is imperfect as all other borrowed tendencies, customs and ideas.

Mimicry of the western cultures constantly appears in India with the pressure of the present times, especially in the domains where the country is incapable of offering its own device. India is not willing to develop its own devices. It is not intellectually equipped for such a development; it is simply used to being guided and unconsciously longs for guidance.

The novelist himself has a very ambiguous position in terms of religious affiliation. Though he clearly states that he is not a believer that he "remained almost totally ignorant of Hinduism" (32) and that his Hindu upbringing evoked only "that sense of the difference of people a vague sense of caste, and a horror of the unclean" (32-33), there was evidently "Hindu-traditional, Brahmin side of him" (Rai 10). It appears in the way he is accepting the people practicing their rituals, in the way he is sympathizing with the Brahmin family and their eating habits and in his ability to "separate the pleasant from the unpleasant" (45).

It is true that Hindu people always tend to escape to their inner world instead of facing the reality. In case of any conflict, they are known for their inactivity. The outer world does not really matter. They live in purity, frugality and non-violence. Poverty is regarded as the part of the Hindu lifestyle. It goes hand in hand with Hinduism, because Hindus are not focused on materialistic aspects of life. It is almost romanticized into something worth adulation.

As the fact of spirituality is concerned Indian are very hypocrite by nature. For them the individual spiritual elevation is superior to the prosperity of the whole nation. The only unit that matters in terms of Hindu lifestyle is caste, clan and family. This deeply established social structure of the Indian social hierarchy. Everyone is predetermined by birth to play a certain role in his life. There is no tolerance of social mobility within caste system. Caste is what primarily defines each person within the society. He writes:

Class is a system of rewards. Caste imprisons a man in his function. From this it follows, since there are no rewards, those duties and responsibilities become irrelevant to position. A man is his proclaimed function. There is little subtlety to India. The poor are thin; the rich are fat. (*An Area of Darkness* 75)

Naipaul finds Indian society living in multiple layers. The society hierarchy of class and caste in India has its roots in *Vedic Period*. According to *Manusmriti*, ancient Indian society was divided into four varnas- "*Brahmins*", "*Kshatriya*", "*Vaishya*" and "*Sudras*". Each was assigned their duty for the better run of the society. Later on, with the passage of time people forgot their duties and remembered their rights only. With the arrival of colonial administration "castes became more apparent". Ursula Sharma in Caste opines that the colonial administration helped to construct the "traditionalism which in their view marked Indian society as backward" (Sharma 8). In this way subalternism is imbibed in the caste structure of India.

In relation to India, caste is treated as an "important component" of the society. Naipaul in his recent visit to India notices the vital role played by caste in constructing social order and in current politics. He is shocked to see the scenes of brutal genocides in the communal riots. Naipaul infers that every invasion in India had strengthened its caste hierarchy. Even the most recent the British, did not try to abolish it, rather they felt "they should make a virtue out of necessity and encourage the formation of classes through the fusion of existing castes" (Sharma 8).

Naipaul focuses on the fragmentation of Indian society in his second visit. Mahatma Gandhi, as he ironically writes, felt the curse of the degraded caste system and tried his best to abolish it by teaching people to "clean the toilets". It was no remedy to him as he failed to abridge the distances between the castes created by the system. He is amazed to see that even after almost three decades of Gandhi's assassination people still feel nostalgic about their clan, caste, race, and religion. In a conventional society like India character and behavior of the people are decided by their caste in which they are born. Thus, Naipaul scorns at this tendency of the society which hinder its inhabitants to go beyond the limitation of their caste. Prestige in India is decided by the birth of a child.

Naipaul does not deplore the caste system as such. He believes that it had a very important role in shaping the nation in the past and it worked well. Yet, he sees the failure of this system as it prevailed into present. The modern society cannot be based on such principles as is caste system and he regards this lasting, deep-rooted social structure as the obstacle on the way to India's transformation and development. He asserts that in the beginning caste system was "useful division of labor in a rural society", but "it has now divorced function from social obligation, position from duties. It is inefficient and destructive; it has created a psychology which will frustrate all improving plans" (*An Area of Darkness* 78).

"*Vernas*" in postcolonial India are converted into class division based on the profession of these people such as "material races", "agricultural" or "non-agricultural" ones. Ursula Sharma points out that colonial rule did not "invent caste" but it "certainly ensured it continued existence and exerted a powerful influence upon its modern form" (Sharma 9). People's obsession with the caste system has given way to the formation of "caste association in urban areas" like Bombay and Madras. According to Naipaul it is gradually destroying humanism and the integrity of India. This hierarchy is responsible for the degradation of mankind, as he expresses in *An Area of Darkness*: in India "it implies a brutal division of labour; and at its centre laid its degradation of the latrine-cleaner. In India caste was unpleasant" (*An Area of Darkness* 34).

Naipaul's observation regarding degraded castes in Hinduism echoes Gandhi's statement regarding 'curse of India'. In his second travel in 1975, he expressed his disgust and anger at the inhuman treatment of '*Harijans*':

Again! Sweepers, the lowest of the low: Their very existence and their acceptance of the function, the special curse of India, reinforcing the Indian connection... that it was unclean to clear. It was unclean even to notice. (*India: A Wounded Civilization* 57)

The upper castes in India do not involve themselves in such 'dirty affairs". Instead, the caste system has created a category of degraded human beings to clean their waste. Naipaul states, "It was the business of the sweepers to remove excrements" (*India: A Wounded Civilization* 57).

This dirt of India was so apparent that it added to his appalling experiences to a great extent.

With his close conversation with a few Dalit leaders, poets, politicians, businessmen and socialites, he again highlights this issue in India, Post-Emergency. In a meeting with the communist Marathi Dalit poet Namdeo Dhasal and his equally popular wife Mallika he further explores the complication of casteism and politics. The disgust and dislike for the traditional system of India and urge to break the shackles of caste gave birth to the outrageous poets like Dhasal. His poems echo the fury of Dalits— "the followers of Dr. Bheem Rao Ambedkar". Naipaul quotes one of Dhasal's translated poems echoing Calibanistic retaliation:

I grow like a person who has lost his fuse.
I ate excrement and grew,
Give me five paise, give me five paise
And take five curses in return.
I am on the way to the shrine. (*Indian: A Million Mutinies Now* 96)

Naipaul concludes this retaliation in consequential of Dalit's awakening. At least, Dalits have tried to break the rigid and irrational norms of their caste which were necessarily not formulated by their ancestors. As a result of Ambedkar's efforts, these rules, which once threatened of their excommunication, are no more followed with the same strictness. Dalits have formed a union known as "Dalit Panthers, a catchy title given by Namdeo Dhasal himself, borrowed from Ameri Negro's union 'Black Panther'. As Naipaul heard vaguely, some years before of the Dalit Panther borrowed from the Black Panthers of United States. It encouraged the – too simpie –belief that the Dalit (or scheduled caste are *harijan* or untouchable were in India what black people in United States" (95).

Caste is one of the most talked about themes among political crisis, poverty, sanitation, social inadequacy and religion etc. in Naipaul' writing. He investigates these themes through history. Dhasal feels reservation and caste promoting policies for Dalits. India cannot leave a major portion of its population in the "darkness of illiteracy" and unemployment. Dhasal tells Naipaul about the condition of untouchable children, who were not allowed to enter the school premises a few years back. Somehow if they managed their admission, they were asked to stand at a reasonable distance from Brahmin children and water sources. Dhasal recollects:

The scheduled caste boys would have to sit outside the school room. They were not allowed to touch any source of water; water had to pour into their cupped hands. A teacher could not touch a scheduled-caste child. When a teacher wanted to punish a child from one of that caste, he threw things at child. (*Indian: A Million Mutinies Now* 113)

Naipaul compares the views of two caste leaders---Dhasal and Mr. Palani. He denotes that both of them vary in opinion regarding Dalit policies but they agree on one point that Indian society is still prejudiced. A child of four or five knows his caste and is duly made aware of his duties if born in a low caste. The elder of these scheduled caste children limit them within the boundaries set by upper caste. Naipaul quotes from one of Namdeo's poem, which laments these sentiments in Namdeo's poems that were completely based of his real-life experiences. His own mother would beat him to keep him in his place. Naipaul writes:

One day he went bathing in a pond with some upper caste boys. The guard spotted him and threw stone at him. He had defiled the pond. He was chased and stoned. He ran bleeding back to his own settlement and hid there. His mother beat him for defiling the pond and causing trouble. (113)

Namdeo Dhasal with a rebellious voice expressed his anger. He feels that to be born in a low caste means to be neglected; it is to born as a non-entity in India. The existence is denied; poverty becomes their undeniable fate. The "holy poverty" in India becomes an inescapable stigma for the untouchables. This curse deepens the chasm between the high and low castes and highlights caste prejudices. This discrimination becomes a kind of regular torture.

In modern India, situations are strengthening caste and politic at the root. A few like Ambedkar tried to fight back these evils in the form of "Dalit movement" which today took an ugly shape of violence. Dalit Marathi poet Namdeo Dhasal states his experiences of caste-based discrimination, "There was a time when we were treated like animals. Now we live like human beings. It is all because of Ambedkar" (*Indian: A Million Mutinies Now* 119).

Shashi Tharoor in *Times of India, Sunday Edition,* writes about Bhimji Rao Ambedkar's caste and his experiences of being an untouchable, "To be born into an "untouchable" family in 1891 of a poor Mahar Subedar in an Army Cantonment, would normally have guaranteed a life of neglected, poverty, and discrimination." Tharoor states that Mahars, the dependents of upper caste, have been living below line since times immemorial. Naipaul writes that Mahars had "the right to call the upper-caste house every day and ask for bread" in return to their duties. It depended on the will of upper caste people to give or to scold. The manner in which they received their bread, itself, speaks of their inhuman status in a society dominated by the upper caste people as "the upper caste people would give bread, letting the bread fall into the basket, without themselves touching the basket" (*A Million Mutinies Now* 114).

Naipaul finds that the condition remains unchanged in certain parts of the country even today. He feels that they are inhuman entities and are deemed to be so forever but by and large their status is rising gradually due to reservation policies promoted and implemented by the efforts of Dr. B. R. Ambedkar. The caste system worked when it was still strong, before 1955. After that it began to break down.

Mahar could be offered money for what they did; but sometimes they were not offered anything. So, while their duties remained the same, such rights as they had begun to diminish. Ambedkar was powerful at that time; and Mahar and other scheduled-caste people began them to make their political demands. (*India: A Million Mutinies Now* 114)

Naipaul also observed that under the reservation policies people took undue advantage of these policies and have become more prejudiced than before. Now the condition has gone out of control and there seems to be no solution for this malady as the modern politics of India uses caste as a major tool. Caste is disintegrating the society. In this relation Shashi Tharoor, in his column *Times of India, Sunday Edition,* May 13, 2007, comments on "the role played by caste in politics as the post-Mandal reservation and the polities of opportunism have preserved the institution into the 21st century, after all in much of rural India, when you cast your vote, you vote your caste."

Naipaul finds that in 21st century, India has become conservative in matters related to caste and religion. People are fighting for reservation quota and have become obsessed with their scheduled-caste and backward-caste status. Caste is the root cause of many evils in India. The only difference is of the attitude which has changed drastically- instead of negative it is the positive discrimination which retains it unhampered even today.

Naipaul's strategy to explore these issues, through a chain of interviews with local party leaders and common people helps to give a factual analysis rather than an official one. Naipaul finds India is still unable to cope with its geo-social-political divide. Role of Shiv Sena and Ambedkarites and local communal forces in the politics of Maharashtra have let the state down.

In *India: A Million Mutinies Now* Mr. Palani, the leader of the backwards in South India, feels grateful to the government reservation policies which enabled him to study in college and be an engineer. He is a weaver by caste. For him caste has proved bliss thus he favours to maintain the caste system. He has arranged all the marriages for his daughters and sons in the same caste. He says, "I became an engineer because of reservation. And I resolved to fight for the similar privileges for others in similar fields" (*India: A Million Mutinies Now* 232).

Naipaul comes to India at a time when the nation is adrift by its social and political crises. The economic situation is shattering due to a high extent of corruption and ineffective governance. His reactions to the country of his origins were shock and despair. The picture of India, which he describes during his first visit, was too severe and cruel for him to be able to maintain an objective eye. Instead, he let all his emotions burst out of him. He could not stand to look at all the squatting people in the dusty streets, ragged, scruffy beggars, and pervasive dirt in the ruins of the long-ago burnt-out glory.

The most striking to the eye for Naipaul, before he could penetrate into the psyche of India, was its visual aspect.

He sees the country full of dirt, dust, starved and sick people and poor beggars. Indian poverty, commented on throughout the travelogue, and it was an enormously painful experience. For Naipaul, "India is the poorest country in the world" (*An Area of Darkness* 44).

Sudha Rai remarks that Ezekiel always quotes Naipaul's negative remarks on India. Ezekiel thinks Naipaul's India "is peopled, packed with a kind of life which is death, a negation, distortion and degradation from which he is gladly finally to escape" (9). Ezekiel quotes Naipaul as saying, on his visit to India, that he is sorry to have had the experience, that it has broken his life in two. The concluding lines show the restlessness of Naipaul after he had visited India first time when he says:

I was a tourist, free, with money. But a whole experience had just occurred; India had ended only twenty-four hours before. It was a journey that ought not to have been made; it had broken my life in two. (*An Area of Darkness* 265)

These are the words V. S. Naipaul writes in the final chapter of *An Area of Darkness*. It was the first time that Naipaul had an opportunity to see the country his grandfather left at the end of the nineteenth century. From the very beginning it is evident that Naipaul is enormously disenchanted with the reality that he has to face during his first sojourn in the country of his ancestors. He "attacks the culture and morality of India both collectively and individually" (Delany 50-51). It is for him a powerful emotional experience, which not only changed his whole life but, above all, it also strongly influenced his further writing.

Naipaul never hesitates in highlighting that beggary has its special position in India and cannot be judged from European perspectives. Beggars have a secure position within the society. It is an inseparable element of India. Beggary has its "function", because every act of "giving to the beggar" is seen as "the automatic act of charity, which is an automatic reverence to God" (*An Area of Darkness*68).

Then the writer reveals another shortcoming of India saying that defecating belongs to India in the same way as beggary. It became almost a ritual. People walk in the streets full of excrements they do not notice, or even see. Although latrines and toilets are still not commonplace in India, the only reason for this situation is that Indians prefer defecating in an open air. It has become their daily routine and habit. For the westerner it is altogether incomprehensible as Naipaul asserts:

Indians defecate everywhere. They defecate, mostly, beside the railway tracks. But they also defecate on the beaches; they defecate on the hills; they defecate on the river banks; they defecate on the streets; they never look for cover. These squatting figures are never spoken of; they are never written about; they are not mentioned in novels or stories; they do not appear in feature films or documentaries. The truth is that Indians do not see these squatters and might even, with complete sincerity, deny that they exist. (70)

Thus, the lineament of culture and civilization are manipulated around the infancy and boyhood of the civilization. But with the passage of time changes is likely to come. In Indian context change has come but this change is utterly unable to supersede the older things. Consequently, the old and new vistas, the old and the new traditions are enjoying a parallel existence. Psychology tells us that the impressions which are erected on the psyche of a child or a boy are difficult to delete at an advanced stage. Likewise, the beliefs and assumptions even practices, which have been coming down to us since the time immemorial are too hard and fast to be broken. Salman Rushdie says rightly, "old habits die hard" (Rushdie 117). It is now mixed in our blood, in our spirit in our "collective consciousness or unconsciousness" (Gussow 46).

In context of India, it is more conspicuous because Indian civilization is the oldest one. There are more paradoxes and contradictory ideologies in it and though there is a professed unity in all its diversity yet reality is indeed different from the apparent one. Naipaul has dexterously brought out such inexplicable and unreasonable disputes concerning Indian civilization and history. But he is only outsider and can see only the external and physical facets and cannot perceive the inner integration. Somehow this inner integration is holding the discrepancies strongly. Jawahar Lal Nehru expatiates upon it:

Though outwardly there was diversity and infinite variety among our people, everywhere there was that tremendous impression of oneness which had held all of us together for ages past, whatever political fate or misfortune had befallen us. The unity of India no longer merely an intellectual conception for me; it was an emotional experience which overpowered me. That essential unity had been so powerful that no political division, no disaster or catastrophe had been able overcome it. It was absurd of course to think of India or any country as a kind of anthropomorphic entity. I was fully aware of the diversities and divisions of Indian life, of classes, castes, religions, races, different degrees of cultural development. Yet I think that a country with a long cultural background and common outlook on life develops a spirit that is peculiar to it and above all that is impressed on all its children however much they differ among themselves. (77-78)

Sometimes Naipaul's judgement is partly correct but at times they are incomplete, vague and indecipherable. It is just because of his inadequate knowledge about Indianness. His constant and recurrent visits to India have acquainted him only with the physical part of India and he remains unacquainted with the inner richness of India. All that Naipaul attempts is to find a reasonable link or relevant meaning among the primary assumptions behind any social custom and its modernized, modified or at sometimes its distorted social manifestations. The actual and relevant purposes and intentions, which have been conceived long ago by the sages and seers, of any ritual ceremony or practices have been desisted long ago. It is Naipaul's limitation that he doesn't stop to explore how and why every ritual ceremony has undergone a gradual change not only in its social manifestation but in its assumed purpose and intention. We can observe here his comments and judgement on some of the oldest and most practiced *sanskars.* For instance, let's have a probe into one short para from his book on India, *An Area of Darkness*:

I had no belief; I disliked religious ritual and I had a sense of the ridiculous, I refused to go through the *janaywa*, or thread ceremony of the newborn with some of my cousins. The ceremony ends with the initiate, his head shaved, his thread new and obvious, taking up his staff and bundle- as he might have done in an Indian village two thousand years ago and announcing his intention of going of Kasi-Banaras to study. His mother weeps and begs his not to go; the initiate insists that he must; a senior member of the family is summoned to plead with the initiate, who at length yields and lays down his staff and bundle. It was a pleasing piece of theatre. But I know that we were in

Trinidad, an island separated but only ten miles from the South American coast and that the appearance in a Port of Spain street of my cousin, perhaps of no great academic attainment in the garb of a Hindu mendicant scholar bound for Banaras would have attracted unwelcome attention. So, I refused, though now this ancient drama absurdly surviving in a Trinidad yard seems to me touching and attractive. (23-24)

Naipaul asserts that he had a sense of ridiculous. Each of the ritual of this thread ceremony is at a time real and meaningful.

Thread ceremony symbolizes the second birth of the already born child. Second birth is supposed to cease the impure life that has gone before. Removing of hair symbolizes the removal of guilty and impure life. The concerned boy takes the pledge of *brahmacharya* and goes for education to *Gurukul* where he lives the life of a mendicant. (*An Area of Darkness* 271-72)

Although much of the syntactic structure of this thread ceremony is in existence and much of the semantic value is extinct now, this ceremony has managed its persistence. Thread ceremony is still much more than a habit. It is a part and parcel of our culture and life. Indians hardly let any of their beliefs and customs die. Indifferent to distorted forms and meaning of this thread ceremony, they show their complete faith to every religious ritual. In spite of appreciating this faith Naipaul restricts himself only to watching over all this as a 'theatre' that is "touching and attractive".

There is a paradox which is preponderant and a strange kind of dilemma in Naipaul's nonfiction. He is always in a fix. He hasn't given a clear impression to his readers whether he is contented with tradition or with modernism.

It is very tough to decide whether he is anti-tradition to pro-tradition. This fix is evidently remarkable in the ensuing pare from the same book:

I had rejected tradition; yet how can I explain my feeling of outrage when I heard that in Bombay, they used candles and electric bulbs for the *Dewali* festivals and not the rustic clay lamps, of immemorial design which in Trinidad we still used? I had been born an unbeliever. Yet the thought of the decay of customs and reverences saddened me when the boy whispered Real brahmin. (*An Area of Darkness* 35)

So as an 'outsider' he can't believe the rites and ceremonies, to name one in particular is the 'thread ceremony' which to Naipaul is a 'theatre' and yet as a Brahmin somewhere lurking within him, he can't approve the changes and alteration in traditional cult. With such a split personality he tries to adjudge the India of 1962 and consequently fails in rendering a complete satisfactory picture of India. In fact, Naipaul's vision of India is biased and colored and defined by too much of the western assumption which obviously gives him a feeling of repulsion rather than attraction for his ancestral homeland.

It is Naipaulian strategy to exploit Indian traditions and culture by using the politics of ethnicity just to get recognition and position in the eyes of western people. He intentionally highlights Indian ethnos with hatred manner knowing no significance of those cultures. Moreover, Naipaul as a traveler on his first visit to India was passing through a very transitional period and was therefore unable to protect correct insights into India or to arrive at the real truth about India. Hence, at the end of the book he almost confessed his failure at grasping the essence of India. He feels he can never adequately express his briefly grasped essence of India.

More he comes nearer to India a queer sort of fear engulfs him. All his experiences and his life in London has taught him a lot but the feeling of reaching nearer to India, the mythical land of his childhood made him slightly uneasy. On the other hand, he himself knows that now he would not be identical himself with India either and in Bombay he finds himself lost in the crowd:

And for the first time in my life, I was one of the crowds. There was nothing in my appearance or dress to distinguish me from the crowd eternally hurrying into Church Gate station. In Trinidad to be an Indian was to be distinctive, in Egypt it was more so. Now on Bombay I entered a shop or a restaurant and awaited a special response. And there was nothing. It was like being denied part of my reality. (37-38)

The real India is completely different from what the author dreamt of as being his homeland. The shock that he has to overcome, when he realizes that the real India has nothing in common with the India of his imagination, is crucial for the overall mood of this book. His family ancestors, who moved to Trinidad, cherished their memories and traditions and it became the source of his ideal thoughts of his mother country.

Nonetheless, Naipaul has very contradictory feelings about his homeland. He feels a very strong bond to this country. His confusion may easily be traced in this book. On one hand, he is distressed of his rootlessness; he does not feel to be an Indian. On the other hand, he is frustrated when he is denied his dissimilarity:

Now in Bombay I entered a shop or a restaurant and awaited a special quality of response. And there was nothing. It was like being denied part of my reality. I had been made by Trinidad and England; recognition of my difference was necessary to me. I felt the need to impose myself, and didn't know how. (43)

The feeling of separateness and disillusion leads Naipaul nearly to a complete negation of India, as it is suggested at the end of the travelogue. "It was only now, as my experience of India defined itself more properly against my own homelessness, that I saw how close in the past year I had been to the total Indian negation, how much it had become the basis of thought and feeling" (*An Area of Darkness* 266). Thus, in his studies and analysis Naipaul appears to make skeptical remark regarding India.

Memory of his past and firsthand experience in time and place, Naipaul could not appreciate India in the way she was appreciated and highlighted in the books he had read. India had always been in his thoughts but gradually it faded and became an area of darkness with no promises to fulfill. That is why in most cases the expatriate writers are in search of 'home'. Unable to find out 'home', they write heaps of papers describing the lands they visit thereby supplying a lot of information including personal ideas to their readers. The post-modern label for those writers haunted by journey motif is 'the rootless searching for roots. The characters in such writings are in most cases seen searching for 'spatial identity'.

In conclusion, it is necessary to remark that Naipaul's deepest hopelessness and despair manifest in *An Area of Darkness*. He cannot cope with the reality that he has to face being for the first time in the land of his forefathers. The real India fails to fulfil Naipaul's expectations. He is absolutely disgusted by the appalling conditions in India. It is the country of dirt and dust. Thus, we see that the west-oriented prejudice is especially obvious in his first book of *India Trilogy*, in which he referred to India as a country in darkness.

In addition to that, the quivering poverty was also very shocking to Naipaul. Wherever he went, he saw dirty districts and poor beggars. It made him feel that he was in the African refugee camp. Poverty made everything in a mess. In the countryside, he saw clusters of shabby houses, lumps of dung, heaps of rubbish and kids shitting everywhere. In the city, he saw overcrowded streets and large area of slums. After the book was published, his description of India had been strongly criticized by Indian scholars, he was even considered as the enemy of the third world countries. Though he succeeded in forcing Indians to face the reality, it was evident that he saw India in the eyes of a westerner. In *An Area of Darkness*, we can see disappointment from the beginning to the end. Moreover, Naipaul's approach of exposing all this is unique.

India: A Wounded Civilization is the second book of the trilogy describing Naipaul's journey to India in 1975. It is evident from the very first chapter that Naipaul's attitudes as well as the style of his narration have changed. Naipaul's flaw is that he confines himself only to the external and visible reality and to the psychological constructions of his childhood. He doesn't try to know the real myth or what the scriptures say but he prefers to give his own interpretation which is at times ludicrous and unintelligible. For instance, Naipaul refers to Goddess Kali in *India: A Wounded Civilization:*

Kali, the black one, the coal black aboriginal goddess surviving in Hinduism as the emblem of female destructiveness, garlanded with human skulls, tongue forever out for flesh blood, eternally sacrificed to but insatiable. (*India: Wounded Civilization 78*)

This statement made by Naipaul shows his immaturity because *Shiv Puran* and other scriptures say that Kali is not garlanded with human skulls but with demon's and evils. Her tongue isn't out for fresh blood but because of her blunder, as she unknowingly kept her foot on the chest of lord Shiva who in order to pacify her rage laid himself down on her path. The sudden revelation gave her a shock because she was his wife Parvati transformed as Kali to annihilate evil from the world. Sometimes Naipaul's honesty is praiseworthy and keeps him always away from hypocrisy but when this non-believer, a great disinterested writer, as uncompromising man feels dejected at the decay of old customs, how can an average Indian go away from the practices and customs, which are in vogue since the time immemorial. But Naipaul satirizes it with sardonic tone:

Customs are to be maintained because they are felt to be ancient. This is continuity enough; it doesn't need to be supported by cultivation of the past and the old, however hallowed be it a Gupta image or a string bed is to be used until it can be used no more. (117-118)

Nevertheless, paradox is not only a part of Naipaul and other great writers but it is a part of every human being, every human civilization, every society and culture. Dr. Sudhir Kakar feels such feelings to be a natural outcome of cultural confrontation:

I have thus aware, in myself and in many other Indian expatriates of a deep and persistent undercurrent of nostalgia, almost sensual in character for the sights, smells, and tastes sounds of the country of our childhood. (50)

India is a country teeming with paradoxes and only an outsider like Naipaul can point it out easily, mercilessly and at times humorously. Indian authors are generally either silent about such drawbacks or they disown these paradoxes. Their imagination abides only by beauty, imaginative or real and by ideology. They never seek the practices of ideology in day-to-day life. How brilliantly Naipaul asserts it:

The prompting is universal, but the Indian practice is purely of India. And do thy duty, if it be humble rather than another, even if it be great. To die in one's duty is life, to live in another's is death. This is the *Gita,* preaching degree fifteen hundred years before Shakespeare's *Ulysses* preaching it today. And the man who makes the dingy bed in the hotel room will be affronted if he is asked to sweep the gritty floor. The clerk will not bring you a glass of water even if you faint. (*India: A Wounded Civilization* 237)

Naipaul says that Indian worship *Geeta,* they kowtow it, even take oath of it in judiciary but they are so much obsessed with the false sense of social stratification and hierarchy that one feels affronted at the encroachment of one's allotted duty. So, the clerk won't bring a glass of water and the stenographer won't type a letter. This is the worst thing and is common in Indian offices and society. Naipaul has rightly observed it. But it can't be applied to all and sundry. There is also a different side of Indian psyche. Naipaul doesn't make any kind of approach to that side. All great personalities have devoted their life in the reformation of such tendencies. It's again a paradox with Indians. They worship and kowtow to their leaders but they try the least to learn something from their imitable life. Every Indian gives his due respect to Gandhiji but the number of his true followers can be counted on fingers. It is admissible that Naipaul presents a true picture, but a disbalanced one. So, there is kind of cultural shock Naipaul feels. It is the same experience Tejaswini Niranjana feels too. She says in one of her books:

I was disturbed to be claimed by some Trinidadian Indians who wanted to mobilize me against the Africans. My book began there, why couldn't I recognize them as Indians? It is because they are part of what India had to cast out in order to become who we are? I began to argue what we have disowned. (*Niranjana 50*)

The description the Islamic culture is also a part of Naipaul's politics of ethnicity because he has used the Islamic values as a writer who just wants to get name and fame without knowing the real significance of those values. He considers that Islam has been changed from century to century. Naipaul is wrong when he says that Islam had the flaw of its origin for not offering a solution to political issues. Naipaul's next statement is that the prophet 'has ceased to exist' is also wrong. To a Muslim this amounts to blasphemy, for spirituality the prophet is always there and every Muslim could always derive the spiritual solace and even guidance that the companions of the holy prophet derived from him. And the final line in which Naipaul makes a sweeping conclusion that 'this political Islam was rage, anarchy.' Obviously, he makes this comment with regard to a particular society in a particular land and to apply this situation to the entire realm of Islam is nothing but a sweeping generalization. However, the most critical and ironical statement against Islam is the following para:

It seemed to me that the deduction might work against them because the massage they were going to take to the world was extraordinary, a divinely inspired prophet, arbitrary rules, a pilgrimage to a certain stone, and a month of fasting. (*Among the Believer* 37-38)

Here by referring to the Haj pilgrimage that a Muslim makes to *Mecca* as a 'pilgrimage to a certain stone' and to Ramjan as a fasting month, Naipaul certainly makes himself appear as a man completely ignorant of the History, the spiritual significance and scientific reasons of fasting to a Muslim.

We see Naipaul's visions of civilization now differ from the existing reality and then it renders a true picture of world civilization. Nevertheless, it must be asserted that it is almost impossible to rely completely on Naipaul's judgement. One single man, of whatever strength, can't know so many different cultures and all it constitutes. He may have a lot of information, through personal interviews and books etc. His consistent and constant sojourns have acquainted him with the external and existing layers of today's life so he speaks of it without taking the inner and integrated matrix into consideration.

Naipaul's vision as a traveller/writer has greater significance in the present context of this study to understand how the writer/traveller documented the culture of the people/places that he had encountered. The ideas conveyed through his narrative bring in the glimpse of 'cultural decay' that had occurred to the civilization and also hints at the social and political conditions prevailing in the country. Hence his travel narratives *India: A Wounded Civilization* and *India: A Million Mutinies Now* are having greater significance in understanding the encounter of culture by the writer/traveller who holds an Indo-Trinidadian identity. Bruce King, critic on Naipaul, comments in *Modern Novelists: V. S. Naipaul*, on the writer's vision of India:

> His criticisms of India are those of a nationalist who feels humiliated by the passivity, factionalism and traditionalism which allowed foreign conquests of India and which contributed to the decay of the great Indian civilization of the past. (King 10)

Naipaul could be seen as keen in his observation on the cultural decay of India. Naipaul's travel narratives on India make the readers analyze the cultural and political changes that occurred to the country after it attained Independence. Purabi Panwar, a critic on Naipaul, remarks about the writer's vision of India, in *V. S. Naipaul: An Anthology of Recent Criticism*, thus:

Naipaul's visit to India will be another way of re-writing the nation for himself. Through his journeys to various corners of the country he will have to see exactly where and how his world view strikes a relationship with his experience in India. (96)

India is a different place for Naipaul. This is the reason why he is able to mentally/physically distance himself with the people and look at them subjectively. Naipaul's point of view could be seen further commented by Mel Gussow thus:

In several cases, including that of his new book, Mr. Naipaul's work has been categorized as travel writing, a label that he accepts as "a portmanteau word." But in no sense is it a book for travellers: it is a book by a traveler. "One is not looking at the sights," he explained. One is exploring the people. I love landscape, but a place is its people. (*New York Times)*

Naipaul does wish to hold on to the racial identity that he had preserved in Trinidad, but it did not have any importance in the Indian context as he felt that Indians did not consider themselves as a single race as they felt the country was divided into smaller kingdoms. The 'negative identity' assigned by the writer to India throughout his travel narratives leads to the conclusion that his expected readers are not Indians, but Westerners. He comments in *India: A Wounded Civilization* thus:

India even absorbs the new into its old self, using new tools in old ways, purging itself of unnecessary mind, maintaining its equilibrium. The poverty of the land is reflected in the poverty of the mind: it would be calamitous if it were otherwise. (*India: Wounded Civilization* 5)

The comment that Naipaul made brands Indians as intellectually poor. This brings in a negative identity for the people even though critic like Bruce King agrees with Naipaul's observation and remarks in *Modern Novelists: V. S. Naipaul* thus:

The world has always consisted of change, it is necessary for people and cultures to adapt. This must however be done creatively, making use of local resources, and with planning and hard work rather than by mimicry of the formal colonial powers. (King 9)

From this comment it could be inferred that cultural development does not occur through unconscious mimicry of the 'other', but it is a conscious and gradual process of 'self' development. Naipaul's vision of India is neither that of a native Indian nor that of a Trinidadian visiting a new/ foreign place. He is a part of India and also was separate from the country. Hence his vision of India is peculiar. Cultural changes occurred in India, but always was a source of imitation of the West as Naipaul narrates in *India: A Wounded Civilization*:

India continues imitative and insecure, as a glance at the advertisements and illustrations of any Indian magazine will show. India, without its own living traditions, has lost the ability to incorporate and adapt: what it borrows it seeks to swallow whole. For all its appearance of cultural continuity, for all the liveliness of its arts of dance, music and cinema, India is incomplete: a whole creative side has died. (*India: A Wounded Civilization* 126)

He is against the idea of using Western yardsticks for studying Indian civilization as observed from *India: A Wounded Civilization*:

European methods of historical inquiry, arising out of one kind of civilization, with its own developing ideas of the human condition cannot be applied to Indian civilization: the European approach elucidates little, has the effect of an unsuccessful attempt to equate India with Europe, and make nonsense of the stops and starts of Indian civilization, the brief flowerings, the long periods of sterility, men forever claimed by the instinctive life, continuity turning to barbarism. (130)

Even though Naipaul claims that European ideologies should not be used as yardsticks for assessing India, he consciously or unconsciously does so. Bruce King comments about Naipaul's views of India that were mixed up with his Western ideologies:

V. S. Naipaul is a rationalist, secular, a strong believer in Western individualism and skepticism, although emotionally attracted towards Indian fatalism, passivity and philosophical notions of the world as illusion. Both world views are together, competing in his writings. (King 5)

This comment highlights that Naipaul's passivity to India and attraction towards the West are due to the competing world views that he had. He is able to give a comparative portrayal of the culture of the two civilizations. The vision of India by foreigners is presented by Naipaul, in *India: A Wounded Civilization*, through the words of middle-class lady in Delhi. She said, "We are like a zoo. Perhaps we should change" (135).

Thus, India is represented by Naipaul based on his individual experiences in the country. Through the trilogy he explores the deep ethnicity that highlights subaltern status of certain castes in India. Naipaul's India series of travel narratives could be seen as shifting its focus from the descriptions of the Indian religion, beliefs etc., to the mannerisms of the people and showing that culture promotes subjugation of humanity in the form of customs and traditions that the people follow. This is explained in the description of the Rajasthani woman. Indian women were presented by the writer as slowly retrieving into their house hold chores as part of their culture.

The voices of the women were muted according to the writer when he had visited Rajasthan. Once again, he observes the subaltern status of women in India. He comments in *India: A Wounded Civilization*, "The women had withdrawn so many of them, below their red or orange Rajasthani veil, only girls, children, but already with children of their own" (30). Naipaul's attention does focus only in a smaller canvas to the women who voluntarily have chosen to live for the welfare of their family.

He does not point at the women who came out of their houses for fighting for India's Independence. This shows that he is selective in his description of the people to show only the subjugation and decay that the people suffered from. It should also be noted that Naipaul's travel narratives on India as such do not give sufficient space for women representations. According to Naipaul, humanity has undergone a lot of change in the present. He comments about this retreat from the past that had happened to Indian civilization, in *India: A Wounded Civilization*:

A retreat from civilization and creativity, from rebirth and growth, to magic and incantation, a retrogression to an almost African night, the enduring primitivism of a place like the Congo, where, even after the slave-trading Arabs and the Belgians. It is the death of a civilization, the final corruption of Hinduism. (King 43)

As it appears from this remark, Naipaul does lack authenticity in documenting about the general behavior of the Indians. Fakrul Alam, critic on Naipaul, in *V. S. Naipaul: An Anthology of Recent Criticism*, strongly opposes such generalized statements of Naipaul. He explains:

Books such as *India: A Wounded Civilization* (1977), *Among the Believers: An Islamic Journey* (1981) and *Beyond Belief* (2001) allshow flashes of brilliance and reveal a master of narrative andshrewd delineator of people and setting, but these are gifts of thewriter of fiction. In his travel writing and exposes of India and IslamNaipaul constantly over states, over generalizes and quite oftenmisrepresents and even distorts what he comes across. (King 192)

This comment highlights the idea that Naipaul might have misrepresented the behavior patterns of the Indians in order to give his travel narrative a fictional touch. This is the point where the objective of writing serious travel narrative often fails in Naipaul. He had to be conscious of the fact that an individual's own set of behavior need not be the same behavior pattern of the whole civilization. It should be seen as purely individual and personal. The defecation of one individual in a public place need not reflect the habit of the whole civilization as Naipaul has depicted.

The third part of the trilogy is considerably different from the first two volumes especially in Naipaul's attitude to India. This travelogue describes India of the late 1980s and the early 1990s. Since the time the author first visited this country India has gone through numerous transformations and reforms and still a great deal of changes is to come. Naipaul observes with the greatest pleasure that India drives itself in a right direction. Although, as he has already suggested, there are still many transformations to be done and the struggle for modern India is not over, it is clear that Indian people had finally woken up from long years of passivity and stagnation.

Naipaul sees India from a much more relaxed point of view. Perhaps the time that passed since his first sojourn in India and the changes that India underwent helped Naipaul to conquer the original feelings of disillusion. It is far more optimistic and it differs very much in style. Naipaul abandons his sophisticated, melancholic comments and reveals the true state of India to the reader through the vivid descriptions of actual people and their stories. He tries to cover the whole social and cultural spectrum of the society. Nonetheless, most of the people Naipaul interviews are men and they are mostly "urban, middle aged, and middle class" (Nixon 110). The author comments on his decision to present India through the interviews with people:

> The idea of letting people talk in the book on the South was really quite new to me. And so, in this book I thought it was better to let India be defined by the experience of the people, rather than writing one's personal reaction to one's feeling about being an Indian and going back – as in the first book *An Area of Darkness* or trying to be analytical, as in the second book. (Nixon 110)

The tone is rather optimistic though in comparison with the two previous books Naipaul leaves much space to the reader to make his own judgments. He does not reveal his attitudes to such an extent. Nevertheless, it is clear that the overall tone of the book is positive.

In *India: A Million Mutinies Now* Naipaul gives an updated account of Indian politics. It reflects the insight of a mature and emotional balanced writer. By now he had already widely travelled India with different guides and local people. More than cultural or economic, it is a social interrogation that forms its chore. He starts from Bombay slum and Muslim dominated areas of the metropolitan. In its first part an attempt to understand the psychology of people deep rooted in their faith and religion is made. Maharashtra, one of India's most developed states, is more deeply marred with communalism and "regionalism" propagated by its regionalism parties like Shiv Sena. The caste and community still decide the shape of the government here. Majority here do not believe in secular ideals of larger groups based on nationalism, consequently India suffered on this front even after more than five decades of independence. Untouchability carries same value and weight for today's politicians as it used to hold in Gandhian era.

Naipaul states the case of a sweeper (low caste born) whom he met during his second visit to India. He feels away with rules of his caste by joining a government job, but Naipaul again found him a sweeper a few years later in his next visit. Naipaul was told by this sweeper boy that he did not want to lose his caste-based identity as he was ex-communicated for disobeying its rule. He believes that the way Indian life is lived it infuses only one ideology – "obedience" sans common sense. He scorns at this ideology and ironically comments that "obedience" is the only thing which "India requires from men and it is what men willingly give" (157).

Naipaul's identity is strongly connected to his imaginary world. With the loss of his ideals, the loss of identity comes immediately. The author feels alienated, not knowing who he really is. He fails to identify with Indians. “In India I had so far felt myself a visitor. Its size, its temperatures, its crowds: I had prepared myself for these, but in its very extremes the country was alien” (140).

The gaze of the foreigners on the Indians is peculiar due to the difference in culture. The rebuke against foreigners by an Indian makes the traveler/writer comment in *India: A Wounded Civilization* thus, “I was a visitor. She intended a rebuke, possibly an insult, but it was easy to let it pass. India was like a zoo because India was poor and cruel and had lost its way” (135).

The reason for the gaze of the foreigners is explained by presenting the land and the people as ‘poor’, ‘cruel’, and ‘lost its way’. Indian civilization has become a show piece in the eyes of the ‘foreigners. The ‘zoo’ imagery used by the writer in his narrative makes the Indian condition worse and pathetic as that of animals.

Cultural chaos was the major backdrop that Naipaul used to portray the decay of Indian civilization. It could be considered as a carefully constructed platform on which he could lay his narrative firmly. India is presented by the writer as a ‘strange’ land without cultural homogeneity to fit to the backdrop of his narration. Naipaul comments about the feeling that he had about India in *India: A Wounded Civilization*:

India, which I visited for the first time in 1962, turned out to be a strange land. A hundred years had been enough to wash me clean of my Indian religious attitudes, and without these attitudes the distress of India was-and is-almost insupportable. It has taken me much time to come to terms with the strangeness of India, to define what separates me from the country: and to understand how far the 'Indian attitudes of someone like myself, a member of a small and remote community in the new world, have diverged from the attitudes of people to whom India is still whole. (*India: A Wounded Civilization* 9)

The 'strangeness' that the writer felt with India was mainly due to his Trinidadian identity. Naipaul's travel narratives could be seen as presenting the writer as distanced from his homeland. His Indian travel narratives are hence an outcome of a purely objective vision of India by the writer without much enquiry into the past of the country. Pratap Bhanu Mehta, in *V. S. Naipaul: An Anthology of Recent Criticism*, talks about Naipaul's vision of India:

In texts such as *India: A Wounded Civilization*, he sees Indian culture as having become one that endlessly repeats its own truisms: even the glorious Vijayanagara was a facile imitation of something that had gone before. Nothing new was possible, because the old was not properly understood. The first thing that strikes most writers on India: its multicultural mélange, its free appropriations, its simultaneous motion in many different directions is of little interest to Naipaul. (Panwar 45)

The 'individual identity' of Naipaul as a traveller visiting India itself is an area of interrogation as he is psychologically detached from India due to the Trinidadian cultural baggage that he carried and is physically attached with India but affected by a 'culture shock'. Still there remains a question about whether Naipaul is the right person to talk about India? This question arises due to his dual Indo-Trinidadian identity. Dileep Padgoankar comments on the genuineness of Naipaul's narration, even though he has a dual cultural identity by citing the examples from *Culture and Imperialism* as evident in *V. S. Naipaul: An Anthology of Recent Criticism*:

In *Culture and Imperialism* Edward Said enlarges upon the idea that the identity of a nation depends on new and different kinds of visions, nations are defined also by their natives who live in exile, the political figure between domains, between homes, and between languages. (Panwar 408)

This comment emphasizes that Naipaul has the right to narrate about India as he has clearer understood about the two cultural domains to which he belongs. It stresses the idea that one's personal opinions of a particular place/ people that he/she visits need not be the view point of the indigenous people in the country. Hence, 'attitude' of the traveller/writer about the people and place, has an important role in the analysis of the travel narratives. Manjit Inder Singh comments on the strangeness that Naipaul felt in India as follows, "Naipaul goes on to elaborate his sides as a man sympathetic to the ways of his family and community yet internally unwilling to participate in its rituals, skeptical and distrustful of other communal groupings" (Singh 190).

This comment shows that Naipaul does distance himself from India knowingly or unknowingly and does not mingle with the people and take part in their religious activities even though his tone of narrative is sympathetic towards the people. The reason for this distancing was the feeling of alienation that the writer had. The strangeness that the writer felt in India had its impact on his travel narratives. Naipaul's narrative is giving clear picture of the conditions of India as seen from the comments of Manjit Inder Singh. In spite of the dislocation or exhaustion that Naipaul felt in India, he was able to give a distinct picture of the Indian culture. A noteworthy point at this juncture is that for all the disillusionment that Naipaul had presented in his travel narratives, India stands as a platform that the writer had already set.

This is a narrative strategy employed by the writer to present social and cultural downfall of India through his travel narratives. The visions of Naipaul can be seen as purely Westernized and unsentimental towards the people whom he is presenting. This observation can be substantiated with the comment of Kate Teltscher, travel critic, in *The Cambridge Companion to Travel Writing*:

The turn towards oral history in *India*: *A Million Mutinies Now* is uncharacteristic both of Naipaul's oeuvre and, more generally, of contemporary travel writing. With the writer's subjectivity centre stage, India usually serves as a backdrop - be it charming, exotic, infuriating, or comic-to the narrator's travels. (194)

From this comment, it could be inferred that India served as the best backdrop to present all the disillusionment that the writer could have. Through the protagonist Jagan, in R. K. Narayan's *The Vendor of Sweets*, Naipaul makes the character voice out the opinion that he had about India as an Indian who experienced the country. Jagan, the character speaks in *India: A Wounded Civilization*, "Why do you blame the country for everything? It has been good enough for four hundred million, remembering the heritage of *Ramayana* and *Bhagavad Gita* and all the trials and sufferings he had undergone to win Independence" (*India: A Wounded Civilization* 33).

This comment by Jagan, the third person in the narrative, is emphasizing that India should not be blamed for everything that happened in the present. The use of the narrative voice of Jagan does fictionalize the travel narratives. Naipaul's narrative ends with an optimistic note for the development of India. He explains in *India: A*

Wounded Civilization, "The past can now be possessed only by inquiry and scholarship, by intellectual rather than spiritual discipline. Past has to be seen to be dead: or the past will kill" (174).

From this comment it could be seen that Naipaul's vision of India is more consolidated and focused on the country's future, predicting the changes that may occur in the civilization in due course, leaving a positive note for the people. But at the same place he is commenting against spiritual discipline and highlights on the need for intellectual scholarship. This is a negative remark on Indian ideologies. Mel Gussow remarked, "The tone of his book signifies a certain mellowing on his part, but it is clear that he is still a man of the most passionate convictions" (Gussow 69).

This view shows that Naipaul had written the Indian travel narratives by keeping a clear intention/motive of what need to be highlighted through his narrative. His travel narratives are especially meant for appealing to the Western readers. Critics like Bruce King are also able to find hidden motives in Naipaul's narrative. He remarks in *Modern Novelists: V. S. Naipaul* thus, "Eventually he found an additional source of income in travelling to and reporting on the social and cultural problems of other parts of the world, especially the newly independent nations" (King 3).

Bruce King aims to say that the motive of Naipaul's narrative could not only be seen as a mode to revive the past history of India but also has a hidden and personal intention. It had also brought him fame and popularity and became a source of income. But these aspects are of less significance considering the real value that the narratives have for the readers in the academic circles as they talk about the culture of a foreign place/people. The personal that Naipaul achieved through his travels is mentioned in *Modern Novelists: V. S. Naipaul* by Bruce King thus:

Such travel corresponded with Naipaul's own need to find new subject matter beyond his memories of Trinidad and provided him with a more interesting life than the solitary existence of a novelist: it contributed to his awareness of the wider world. (3)

Through the representation of the attitude of a small section of people, Naipaul is misrepresenting the Indian civilization as a whole. This is purely a Western attitude that the writer had. Billie Melman remarks in *The Cambridge Companion to Travel Writing* thus, "Real orientals are denied humanity, history and the authority to speak about and represent themselves, an authority which Orientalist travel writing reserves for occidentals" (Melman 107).

Naipaul says that the knowledge of the country changes the identity of the citizen. This shows that identity is related with culture as the individual has an individual and collective identity of which he/she is a part. What Indians lacked in the present context of the narrative is the sense of 'collective identity' of being part of the Indian civilization. Most of the Indians are presented by the writer/traveller as unaware of the historical past of India. Bhanu Pratap Mehta disagrees to this point in *V. S. Naipaul: An Anthology of Recent Criticism* and remarks:

In *India: A Wounded Civilization,* Naipaul's chief concern was the lack of proper historical awareness. He insistently attributes this intellectual depletion to centuries of conquest for Naipaul conquest's chief achievement is to distort historical consciousness. European colonialism had at least this redeeming feature: it began to impart an inchoate sense of Indians to India's own inadequacies, but it produced no intellectual movement that could allow India to transcend those adequacies. (Panwar 45)

His travels were the attempts to understand more about his ancestry and about the culture to which he belongs. This observation could be asserted from the comments of Peter Hulme in *The Cambridge Companion to Travel Writing*, "Subsequently, in no fewer than three travel books of increasing complexity, Naipaul has written about India, a country he returns to at least in part for complex reasons of personal heritage" (Hulme 89).

Naipaul was able to make a detailed analysis of the culture and tradition of Indian society through his travels. The knowledge that he gained of such an inquiry could be seen as entirely contradictory from the glory of which India could boast off. He remarks in the interview published in *V. S. Naipaul: An Anthology of Recent Criticism*:

The essence of literature, inquiry and philosophy is a constant examination of oneself and one's world and one's own culture. One hopes to leave the world with different ideas than those given to one when one enters the world. (Panwar 56)

This comment emphasizes that India had an entirely different picture when Naipaul was about to leave the country. This picture of India was different from the already existing notions that he had when he entered the country. Kate Teltscher comments in *The Cambridge Companion to Travel Writing* about Naipaul's response to India:

In twentieth-century texts particularly those published after independence in 1947, India offers a site for the interrogation of the writer's own identity. This is obviously the case with the Trinidadian-born British resident V. S.

Naipaul who over three books and nearly thirty years chronicled his response to Independent India. (Kate 194)

Naipaul is providing a negative representation about the Indian politics through his travel narratives in the backdrop of the mutinies that India suffered. He feels that the Gandhian principles were completely misunderstood by the people. He comments in *India: A Wounded Civilization* thus:

Gandhian non-violence has degenerated into something very like the opposite of what Gandhi intended. It is non-doing, non-interference, social indifference. It merges with the ideal of self-realization, truth to one's own identity. The acceptance of Karma, the Hindu killer, the Hindu calm, which tells us that we pay in this life for what we have done in past lives, so that everything we see is just and balanced, and the distress we see is to be relished as religious theatre, a reminder of our duty to ourselves, our future lives. (25)

Fragmented notions that Naipaul had about India's colonial past and the misinterpretation of the mutinies that Indians had suffered were the major drawback in his narratives. He is presenting an entirely different picture of non-violence in the present Indian context as 'non-doing', 'non-interference' and 'social indifference'. 'Karma' or the moral obligation of the people is also misrepresented in the narrative as the 'Hindu Killer'. The real value of Ahinsa is casually forgotten by the writer while viewing it in the context of 'cultural decay'.

Indian culture is misinterpreted through the description of the Indian belief in Karma which is presented by Naipaul in a new version as 'parasitic' and as a response of India's 'defeat' to the external world. India is provided a new negative identity through the representation of Indian ideologies. The failure of Gandhian ideas to provide an identity for the Indians is seen as a major factor that has affected Indian culture as he narrates in *India: A Wounded Civilization*:

If he had projected on to India another code of survival, he might have left Independent India with an ideology, and perhaps even with what in India would have been truly revolutionary, the continental racial sense, the sense of belonging to a people specifically of India, which would have answered all his political aims, and more: not only weakening untouchability and submerging caste, but also awakening the individual, enabling men to stand alone within a broader identity, establishing a new idea of human excellence. (174)

Naipaul makes a derogatory comment on Indian spirituality which according to him has swallowed up and annulled that very civilization of which Indians boast. Naipaul's conclusions are for from logic and intelligibility. Only Naipaul concludes that the entire life of Bhave is a fiasco. The highly tempoed and much hyped prank of his 'land-gift' scheme for which he appeared on the cover of *Time Magazine* to Naipaul, is a wild goose chase. Bhave's almost inhuman walk throughout the country with innumerable followers is simply a crowd to Naipaul creating a circus like atmosphere, din, shout, belching, hawking and farting. And Naipaul concludes:

Magic hadn't worked; spirituality hasn't brought about land distribution to more importantly the revolution in social attitudes that such redistribution required. The results had been the opposite. Bihar where Bhave did much of his walking remains in matters of land and untouchability among the most backward and crushed of the Indian states. (*Indian: A Wounded Civilization* 117-118)

Naipaul also says that Bhave is not a particular intelligent man and as a perfect disciple of the Mahatma. Above all Bhave was not a political man, but a saint of Indian heritage and tradition devoted to social reform. He was innovative in the land gift scheme and any innovation comes only from men of intelligence and will. Naipaul should have appreciated for his genuine efforts rather than counting his success and failures. Land-gift scheme wasn't a total failure. Numberless people were given land that brought the succour to them. Like happiness, goodness is also an occasional episode in the general drama of life. It cannot persist for long but this should not imply that human being should desist from efforts that may be beneficial for the prosperity. Why only Bhave, if the aftermath is to be judged and taken into consideration, almost all great visionaries are to be questioned viz. Plato, Socrates, Buddha, Nanak, Martin Luther King, Gandhiji etc.

Does Naipaul mean to say all of them are worthless because they have not left a lasting impact on the psyche of common mob? This is undue tyranny on the intellectual level. It is a part of occidental strategy that has been described by Edward Said in *Orientalism*. Orientalism refers to the sum of West's representation of the orient as a "timeless place, changeless and static irrational" (Said 89). Said further states that the western travelers perpetuate commonly held opinions and assumptions about the orient as a "mythic place of exoticism, moral laxity, and sexual degeneracy" etc. Exactly in the same way Naipaul in the last few pages sums up:

It seems to be always there in India, magic, the past, the death of the intellect, spirituality annulling the civilization out of which it issues. India is swallowing its own tail. (*India: A Wounded Civilization* 134)

Bruce King's comment shows that Naipaul's opinions and observations on India has to be re-examined by the readers before setting an identity on India and its people. This is because he is unable to position himself within the Indian and Trinidadian identity. Had all this been true in its entirety, how can one assume where India would have been? One must be on his guard while going through such phases of recreation of History by Naipaul. This may be in starkest contrast with the common historical perspectives. In fact, it is not a recreation of history but a distortion of history. Since history cannot be recorded on the basis of sparse evidences that are cut off from their context but on the basis of evidence that are consolidated by various sources. Comparing Naipaul's treatment of history with one of his contemporaries Salman Rushdie, Khan rightly observes:

Salman Rushdie has treated history in his novels like *Shame* and *Midnight' children* in such a way as to bring the past in close juxtaposition to the present but Naipaul has made use of history in order to recreate the past for the review of the present which serves to throw light on the similarity or difference of attitude of the people towards identical situation. (112)

The colonial traumatic situations culminated in the multifaceted sensibility of Naipaul with which he veered towards India and other third world countries to know the veracity of the much-boasted glory and richness of culture; but being trained in the western academic and critical ambience he developed a vision which could reach only to visible things. And visible India is 'filth, din, dust and 'an area of darkness.' This hatred and contempt for one's own people and culture is also known to Frantz Fanon:

At a given stage (such a writer) feels that his race no longer understands him, or that he no longer understands it. Then congratulating himself on grasping this fact, he enlarges the difference, the disharmony, the incomprehension and finds in them the meaning of this real humanity. (Fanon 16)

Having this premise in consideration Fawzia Afzal Khan in *Cultural Imperialism and Indo English Fiction*, in the introduction concludes:

In doing so Naipaul creates a literature of self-hatred that duplicates orientalist strategies of containment in which myth is used neither to debunk itself nor glorify the past, but as a symbol of petrified societies enshrouded in perpetual darkness. (Khan 11)

The visual aspect of the country improved as well. There are far fewer squatting beggars in the streets, not because there would not be any in India, but because, for the author, they are not as symbolic for India as they used to be. Poverty of people is not that shocking and the conditions of living ameliorate with every new day.

Naipaul is very much concerned with the changes in social structure. Caste system still exists in India, but the Indian people are aware of a necessity to release its bonds. Among the interviewed people there are those who do not care about their caste at all. Hinduism still has a very powerful role within the country because Indians have always been deeply religious people but even the Hindu traditions go through substantial changes to satisfy the needs of modern society.

People start to be focused on their individual needs and the spiritual world that used to be the core of their existence is replaced by the materialistic world. The achievement of self-awareness and individuality is seen as the predisposition for the development of the nation and creation of national identity. "India has entered a state of regenerative disintegration" (Nixon111). Indians like people in other countries strive hard to improve their standard of living. Education is very important for them and many young people go to finish their studies at the universities abroad. The position of women in the society gets better. Women are no longer seen as mothers, whose only target is bringing up their children. They start to build their own careers.

Naipaul uses the term "million mutinies" for the strife of individuals against long ago established social and cultural norms. The individuals in India feel the need to change their country and India is full of small riots on the basis of individuals and small groups of people.

A million mutinies, supported by twenty kinds of group excess, sectarian excess, religious excess, regional excess: the beginnings of self-awareness a central will, a central intellect, a national idea. The Indian Union was greater than the sum of its parts. (*India:* A *Million Mutinies Now* 517-518)

People had a little more money now. Indian poverty was still visible, the maidens, the broken-down aspect of houses and lanes, but the fields of sugar-cane and cotton and other crops looked rich and well-tended. The village houses were often neat with plastered walls and red-tile roofs. There was nothing like the destitution he had seen 26 years before when he had travelled through on a slow, stopping bus. There were none of the walking skeletons with their deranged eyes. He says:

The agricultural revolution was a reality here; the increased supply of food showed. Hundreds of thousands of people all over India, perhaps millions of people, had worked for this for four decades, in the best way: very few of them with an idea of drama or sacrifice or mission, nearly all of them simply doing jobs. (*India:* A *Million Mutinies Now* 149)

As apparent from the extract above, the living conditions in India extensively improved. The situation is still not ideal, but in comparison with the situation described in the previous two books of the trilogy, the poverty manifests itself in a much more suppressed form and the living standard of people increased. This is due to the changes in people's thinking. The materialistic aspects of their lives gained considerable importance. With the introduction of new technologies, the condition of people's everyday affairs is much easier. What used to be seen as the craze of people of higher social status and the manifestation of power and wealth several years ago, slowly but surely becomes the necessity and commonplace for a larger scale of Indian social spectra.

Because of industrialization, and the green revolution in the rural areas, a new class of nouveau riche persons is emerging, and these people are being exposed for the first time to university education, comfortable urban life, stylish living, and western influences – materialistic comforts. During this transition period, we are slowly cutting from the moral ethos of our grandfathers, and at the same time we don't have the westerner's idea of discipline and social justice. (*India:* A *Million Mutinies Now* 189)

Naipaul broadly writes about many reforms running through the country in agriculture, industry and living standard. He describes the electrification in villages, irrigation system in agriculture and sanitary improvements of the slums. The Indian scientific growth and development is no less important. India is slowly recovering from its failures. The intellectual capacity of the country is increasing and the new technological centers are established like space research and aircraft industry in Bangalore. "Every kind of scientific institution was in Bangalore" (*India: A Million Mutinies Now* 150).

There is a significant reform in women's position within the society. Women care about their education and careers. A relevant step afore for the strengthening of their position within the society is the publication of women's magazines and newspapers such as *Woman's Era, Eve's Weekly* or *Femina*. There were no Indian women's magazines before independence. Middle-class Indian women "read the two popular British magazines, *Woman's Weekly* and *Woman's own*. When the British went away these magazines ceased to be available" (*Million Mutinies* 406-407).

Most of the marriages in India are still being arranged. Nonetheless, the number of "love" marriages is mounting. Foreign marriages also become common or at least more frequent in contemporary Indian environment. Although the living conditions, the position of women in the society and the economic situation are still not equal to developed countries, India slowly but surely follows their direction.

As Indian society is deeply religious, Hinduism cannot be considered merely as a religion in India, it is rather a lifestyle. It determines and transfuses into every aspect of Indian life and, in its traditional form, it has put an obstacle on the Indian way to progress. Therefore, as Naipaul has already stated that the traditional religious and social principles of the Indian society have gone through radical changes. Although Hindu religion cannot be completely diminished, which is not even necessary, it becomes more fitted to the needs of the contemporary economic development of the Indian society. "Everybody tries to change things to suit himself. The rituals were being adapted all the time" (*India:* A *Million Mutinies Now* 56). Some of the old traditions and rituals perished and those, which survived, were transformed to better serve the needs of the individuals. From the previous two books it is clear that most of the rituals practiced in India are not fully understood by Indians themselves and with every new generation they are losing their meaning.

It might have seemed then that Hindu India was on the verge of extinction, something to be divided between Christian Europe and the Muslim world, and all its religious symbols and difficult theology rendered as meaningless as the Aztec gods in Mexico, or the symbolism of Hindu Angkor. But it hadn't been like that a Hindu India had grown again, completer and more unified than any India in the past. (*India:* A *Million Mutinies Now* 143)

The caste system as a social order in India is still prevailing, but Many protests run through the whole country and the new attitudes are shaped. Naipaul broadly describes the Dravidian movement against Brahmins and their traditions initiated by Periyar:

Other middle castes began to produce their own prominent personalities. Many of these middle-caste people were well-to-do . . .. Many were landlords; some could send their sons to Oxford and Cambridge. As soon as such people had emerged from the middle castes, the antique Brahmin caste restrictions would not have been easy to maintain. What Periyar did was to take this mood of rejection to the non-Brahmin masses. (*India:* A *Million Mutinies Now* 223)

Fawzia Afzal Khan explains it as self-hatred of Naipaul. This self-hatred drives him incessantly to demarcate the difference between what he is today (an inhabitant of the world of light) and what his very distant past (with its link to India) was (a world of darkness). What he is today- he repeats obsessively throughout the book—is an Anglicized West Indian with a remote Indian ancestry with the emphasis on Anglicized.

Caste system is still defining people's position in the country. Indians are not able to completely withdraw from their long-ago established caste system. It became too much part of their identity. Though, the approach of individuals slightly modified, caste is still determining for certain positions and functions.

Caste was the first thing of importance. A man looking for office or a political career would have to be of a suitable caste. That meant belonging to the dominant caste of the area. He would also, of course, have to be someone who could get the support of his caste; that meant he would have to be of some standing in the community, well connected and well known. (*India: A Million Mutinies Now* 187)

The writer's initial sensation of despair and disillusion is gone and warm-hearted feelings and the reconciliation with the country come. V. S. Naipaul negotiated a long journey from 'darkness' since his first encounter with India. Although India will never be his home, a very strong sympathy grew in him in almost thirty years of his Indian cognition. "In 27 years, I had succeeded in making a kind of return journey, shedding my Indian nerves, abolishing the darkness that separated me from my ancestral past" (516).

Naipaul's alienation from the country of his origins as well as from the country of his birth still lasts; nevertheless, it is clear that the author learned to benefit from his own position within the world. He claims that England is the country where he mostly feels at home. Yet for the rest of the English population, he is an Indian in England and for Trinidadians he is an Indian born in Trinidad. He is simply redeemed with his uniqueness and his trilogy itself supports the idea that his uncertain position provides him with the superb, matchless outlook to the outside world.

Therefore, it is necessary to remark that the ideas mentioned in *An Area of Darkness* form the concept for Naipaul's further works India: *A Wounded Civilization* and *India: A Million Mutinies Now.* The author deals with the same ideologies in all three books, but with different attitudes, which are shaped through his own experience. There is a certain progress in formulating his ideas and the author's perspectives change with every single book. Relatively broad period of time, when the trilogy was written, suggests its diversity in style and sentiments. The author's disillusion is the principal idea unifying the trilogy. Yet it is obvious that the initial disillusion that Naipaul feels when he first comes to India modifies into certain reconciliation with the country of his ancestors as well as with his self. He finally comes to terms with India and concurrently with his own deteriorated identity. India has always been a place of many different tendencies and ambiguities for Naipaul. He both feels the strong bonds with this country and tries to untie himself at the same time. The confusion he feels when he first comes to India substantially affects his apprehension of the country. But the inceptive bewilderment changes into sympathy and better understanding of his ancestral country.

It is this emotional aspect that differentiates Naipaul's travel books from typical travelogues. The author projects himself to his narration and the attitudes towards India can be considered as solely his own response to the country. As was already stated, he reveals not only Indian situation but his own personality as well. This is perhaps why the interpretations of this trilogy vary in certain aspects. They agree on the central idea of Naipaul's disillusion and alienation, nonetheless, they differ in the extent. For example, Sudha Rai accentuates Naipaul's warm-hearted relationship to India even in what she considers the most pessimistic book of the trilogy *An Area of Darkness*, whereas Peggy Nightingale rather leans to more depressive version of interpretation.

Naipaul's deepest hopelessness and despair manifest in *An Area of Darkness*. He cannot cope with the reality that he has to face being for the first time in the land of his forefathers. The real India fails to fulfill Naipaul's expectations. He is absolutely disgusted by the appalling conditions in India. It is the country of dirt and dust.

In *India: A Wounded Civilization*, Naipaul is even more severe in his descriptions, because they are freed from emotions. It is more analytical and objective. He stays focused on the same topics as in the first book. Although his narration is full of stern indictments, in the end, he reveals a sense of hope and believes in Indian ability to transform their country.

India: A Million Mutinies Now is the last and the most positive volume of the trilogy. It is written in the form of interviews. Naipaul provides the reader with the description of India through real experience of Indian people. He tries to avoid his commentaries. The living conditions of people largely improved, the agriculture and industry increased their production. The traditional caste system and Hindu traditions are slowly but surely losing their power. India is finally moving ahead.

This book astonishes its readers because of the brighter, deeper and more lucid picture of India. Of course, the dark background is not wholly absent but these dark clouds are not without the silver lining. Moreover, the utter bleak and fragmented picture that he had depicted in his earlier books is no longer here, in the contrary his vision of India seems to have changed substantially. We find now that along with decay, frustration, rebellion and mutinies, Naipaul notices in the intellectual life of India a deep consciousness of wholeness and humanism which make it altogether a book with a difference. Such perception of India projects his recognition of values, a humanism he had earlier denied to India.

Nevertheless, the most remarkable feature of this book lies in the fact that Naipaul expresses his views on sensitive subjects indirectly through his various characters rather than himself. Thus, Naipaul recedes into the background and makes his characters express their views which clearly stand to support and reiterate the author's view expressed in his earlier books.

Therefore, conclusion may be easily made that Naipaul's trilogy portrays India in a new way, though there are certain familiar shades. The entire world experiences a new India in this trilogy and comes to know about its great political leader in a different way. Authenticity is one criterion that abrogates much of Naipaul's judgment but Naipaul has done one thing superbly. He had shown the practiced reality of India in its utter nakedness and the hollowness of professed ideology of Indian *karma, dharma* and *moksha.*

The main focus of Naipaul in his trilogy has been to present the subaltern voices of every section of Indian prevailing in our society, be it dalit, women, workers, caste-class divide, gender discrimination or women and voiceless people. Through the caste system Naipaul has exposed the hypocrisy of Indian people and the degrading condition of dalits caste people and women. The writer seriously questions about the injustices meted out to the marginal people and the hypocrisy of India. After all, Naipaul's efforts to highlight the muted voices of real people of the nation are praiseworthy. All this has been done by Naipaul through the personal interviews taken by the writer. This effort of Naipaul will remain as a milestone in this process.

Works Cited

Allardt, E. "Implications of Ethnic Revival in Modern Industrialized Society: A Comparative Study of the Linguistic Minorities in Western Europe." *Comminutions Scientrarum Socialism*. Ed. J. N. Tailor.Helsinki: Scientarum Fennica, 1979. Print.

Bell, Daniel. "Ethnicity & Social Change". *Ethnicity: Theory and Experience*. Eds. N. Glazer & D. P. Moynihan. Cambridge: Harvard University Press, 1975. 141-174.

Burnett, Edward Tylor. *Primitive Culture*. New York: Holt, 1877. Print.

Fanon, Frantz. *Black Skin, White Masks*. New York: Grove Press, 1967. Print.

Gussow, Mel. "The Enigma of V. S. Naipaul's Search for Himself in Writing." *New York Times*. 25 April, 1987. Print.

---. "Travel Plus Writing Plus Reflection Equals V.S. Naipaul." T*he New York Times*. http://query. my times. com/gst/fullpage.html? January 30, 1991.

--- . *Writer Without Roots*. New York: Vintage, 1976.

Hulme, Peter. *The Cambridge Companion to Travel Writing*. London: University of Essex, 2002.Print.

Khan, Fawzia Afzal. *Cultural Imperialism and Indo-English Fiction*. New York: OUP, 1995. Print.

King, Bruce. *V. S. Naipaul*. London: Macmillan, 1993. Print.

--- . *Modern Novelist: V. S. Naipaul.* London: Macmillan Press, 1989. Print.

Kipling, Rudyard. *Best of Attack and National Vangard.* London: The National Alliance, 2005. Print.

Niranjana, Tejaswini. *Mobilizing India: Women, Music and Migration Between India and Trinidad.* North Carolina: Duke University Press, 2006. Print.

Panwar, Purabi. *V. S. Naipaul: An Anthology of Recent Criticism.* Delhi: Pencraft International, 2003. Print.

Riggs, Fred. W. *Ethnicity: Intercocta Glossary, Concepts and Terms Used in*

Ethnicity Research 4. Paris: Hawai SocialScience Council, UNESCO, 1985. Print.

Teltscher, Kate. "India/Calcutta: City of Palaces and Dreadful Night." *The Cambridge Companion to Travel Writing.* Eds. Peter Hulme and Tim Youngs. Cambridge: Cambridge University Press, 2002. Print.

CHAPTER THREE

In a Free State and A Bend in the River: The Psychology of Marginalization in Diasporic Location

This chapter discusses Naipaul's dealing with the psychology of marginalization of characters in diasporic location. They are described as fragile and powerless, trapped in the political atmosphere associated with the transfer of power at the advent of decolonization. The idea of rootlessness is one of Naipaul's common themes in his writings. The negative aspect of the idea of rootlessness dominates in his writings. Contrary to the characters' expectation to satisfy their desire for freedom in foreign countries, their freedom is denied because of the political condition. Their sense of imprisonment is also depicted spatially. For instance, their living space is often fortress guarded from the indigenous population. Furthermore, such spatial depiction generates an atmosphere of separation with the expatriate characters removed from the indigenous population, reflecting Naipaul's pessimism about cultural interaction in the postcolonial era.

Diasporic writing captures the two invariable of their experiences: exile and homeland. All diasporic literature is an attempt to negotiate between these two polarities. The writings of exiled/immigrant writers undertake two moves, one temporal, and one spatial. It is, as Meena Alexander puts it, "writing in search of a homeland" (4).

The diasporic characters in Naipaul's writings are depicted as being deprived of man's essential needs of independence and freedom and having restrictive lives because of the politically unstable situation. In Naipaul's writings the sense of displacement gives rise very profoundly to a certain imaginary plenitude, recreating the endless desire to return to lost origins, to go back to the beginning. And this return to the beginning can neither be fulfilled nor requited, and hence is the beginning of the symbolic of representation, the infinitely renewable source of desire, memory, myth, search and discovery. Sometimes this search and discovery or rediscovery of land in a terrain of anxiety, ecstasy and frustration as the very individual or author discovers the homeland different from what he had been dreaming of and what he had been told of the purity of the homeland.

V. S. Naipaul has this discovery as his recurrent theme. So, the core genesis of perception and understanding behind the realm of a diasporic writing or diasporic discourse of Naipaul principally relates to the historical and socio-cultural junctures. He has given some dimensions through which the populace of a country has undergone alteration and transformation in the critical process of immigration, adoption and the kind of inner conflict and tension germinating out of this critical process.

Diasporic consciousness, exilic self and the resultant sensibility that stands as the core genesis to cross-cultural or expatriate or diasporic discourse or writing is the perspective through which Naipaul's relationship and affiliation with India needs to be studied and analyzed. Most prominently, diasporic consciousness is being perceived as the mental flights of a people, who are in continual pursuit of reconstructing their present from a past that is lost to them.

Stuart Hall in his attempt to define diaspora and diasporic identity claims that "diaspora does not refer to those scattered tribes whose identity can only be secured in relation to some sacred homeland to which they must at all costs return, even if it means pushing other people into the sea" (159). Discussing and analyzing the hybridity and heterogeneities in diasporic identities, which are constantly producing and reproducing themselves a new through transformation and difference, Hall goes on to claim that it is because this New World which is constituted for us as place, a narrative of displacement that gives rise so profoundly to a certain imaginary plentitude, recreating the endless desire to return to "lost origins", to be once again with the mother, to go back to the beginning.

Diasporic literature can be viewed as the area for negotiating and contesting for self-fashioning and refashioning. It emerges as a counter discourse which fictionalizes '*otherness*' and '*difference*' in the context of self and environment. Diasporic writings present dual perspectives that of the insider as well as the outsider. These writers have come out of 'closed' mentality and address the world that lies outside their respective communities and geographical boundaries. This aspect of diasporic literature makes it enduring and worthwhile. Its multicultural and pluralistic outlook makes it truly universal and appealing.

Diaspora refers to a community of individuals living outside their homeland, who identify themselves in some way with the state or people of that homeland. The components of a diasporic identity are a history of dispersal, memories or myths of a homeland, ongoing interest in the homeland, retaining sense of its uniqueness, alienation in the host country, and desire for an eventual return to the homeland. Judith Shuval stresses:

A diaspora is a social construct founded on feeling, consciousness, memory, mythology, history, meaningful narratives, group identity, longings, and dreams, allegorical and virtual elements all of which play an important role in establishing a diaspora reality. At a given moment in time, the sense of connection to a homeland must be strong enough to resist forgetting, assimilating or distancing. (43)

Diaspora is not just a matter of possessing multiple identities as putting on different cultural faces. What distinguishes diasporic people is their ongoing attachment and persistent loyalty to their earlier culture and specifically the homeland that they feel they have left. Ien Ang insightfully defines diaspora as "a concept of sameness-in-dispersal, not of togetherness-in-difference" (13). With the notion of the cosmopolitan as an identity-less or rootless citizen of the world, the old cosmopolitanism rejects the view that every man belongs to a community among communities. It marks a sensibility that transcends the provincialism and absolutism of singularly construed ethnic, racial, and especially national identities. It does not fully allow for the continuing importance of country of origin and ethnic ties in migrant networks. The diaspora, though in a similar rootless and unattached condition like the elite cosmopolitan, is doubly misguided because of its dual loyalties or disloyalty to the country of settlement.

The literature of diaspora revolves around the concept of homeland, which has been variously defined in different generation of diaspora writers. The construction of homeland in the writings of the diasporic writers depends upon their category to which they belong. In the case first category that is the older diaspora we see dysconnectivity with the motherland due to the lack of economic means to make frequent journeys to the homelands. The distance of their motherland was more psychological than physical and it was wide that the motherland remained unnoticed in the diasporic imagination. The distance was revived by the emotional and spiritual in the writings of the older diaspora writers revitalizing memory and imagination. Vijay Mishra talks about the process of connecting to the lost homeland in V. S. Naipaul:

The narrative of diaspora movement is, however, not continuous or seamless as there is a radical break between the older diasporas of classic capitalism and the mid-to late 20th century diasporas of advanced capital to the metropolitan centers of the Empire, the new world and the former settler colonies. (56)

As mentioned in the introduction that the postcolonial literature includes the literature produced by the countries affected by colonial process. It refers to a "historical phase undergone by Third World countries after the decline of colonialism" (Boehmer 166). The colonized writer in diaspora texts maintains the standard mimic responses—while appealing as the "other". In these writings "colonial claimed interpretation agency, centre v/s margin relationships were disturbed" (Boehmer 166). Writers living in exile possess this quality. The past history of a writer plays a significant role in nostalgic writings. His birthplace, education, cultural roots, community and tradition affect his writings. Living in an alien land he finds himself uncomfortable and dislocated. Nostalgic writings give him solace and help him to overcome such dilemma.

Naipaul expressed his view that after 1950s the societies everywhere have been fractured drastically by change. The whole world now requires another kind of imaginative interpretation. So, keeping this fact in mind, the writer made an attempt to give a new interpretation of society. The novel *In a Free State*, which was published in the year 1971, portrays fractured postcolonial societies in which everyone is becoming an "exile," cut off from a community of others, at the mercy of the illogical laws of a dictator or the lawlessness of revelries. The breakdown depicted on Naipaul's1970s novels refers to a political and socio-economic "free state" into which countries of sub-Saharan African and other region of the developing world are falling or have already fallen.

In a Free State has an objective approach to deal with the problem of colonial subjugation. In this book Naipaul probes into the paradoxical nature of freedom which instead of liberation the colonial subjects only make them casualties of freedom. It is written in fragments. Champa Rao Mohan calls it "the structural deformity" (98) but it could be undermined due to the "fragmented nature of the world it co-operates." *In a Free State* consists of a "Prologue" and "Epilogue" along with two short stories and a novel titled *In a Free State*. These pieces are associated with the "concept of freedom." They examine the concept of freedom in its political, social and psychological dimension. Bruce King remarks that it is one of those three novels which "are rich in psychology, in awareness of how insecurity is transformed into violence and tyranny" (King 83). In this novel particularly, Naipaul has projected how emotions defeat the people and compel them to "repeat the same behavior." The personal lives illuminate the political world without stability or purpose, people are lost and trying to search the way out.

Naipaul's third world is fictional, though, as well as factual. *In a Free State* describes an East African country falling apart that is a combination of Rwanda, Uganda, Kenya, and Trinidad. The Caribbean Island of Guerrillas is a fictional Trinidad; the Central African country of *A Bend in the River*. It is a mixture of Zaire, Uganda, and again Trinidad. From a literary perspective, there is a sense in which all of these places are images of a single, fictional state, a fourth world of fear, the menace of violence and horror. This vision of fourth world derives in part from European colonial discourse about sub-Saharan Africa, especially from Conrad's stories set in "half-made societies" forever making and unmaking themselves. It derives from a particular ideological realm and literary-language consciousness, from a myth that exists before Naipaul in his novels, is reshaped by his colonial background, exile, and travels in the Third World, in conjunction with the historical contexts of the 1960s and 1970s.

The main characters in the diaspora texts are mostly outsiders, exiles or alienated minorities— those who are uprooted from their origins, travelers without a home to return, minorities at the mercy of others, those stranded by the withdrawal of protecting governments, former enemies brought together by the artificial boundaries of the new nations, and also those who have to come to the capital of the world without the necessary skills and resources to survive. They all have to suffer alienation and establish a new order in the world, called a subaltern in a diasporic location. They all seek freedom from the past and freedom from identity crisis. But they are also bound to undergo the dangers that freedom brings. Bruce King argues in *V. S. Naipaul:*

If the modern world freedom is dangerous, there are also signs of new empires, new orders-the seemingly innocent Americans confidently traveling abroad, the Chinese traveling in tightly controlled groups. Naipaul examines the Europeans who come to former colonies seeking careers or personal salvation, the dangers to the Indian diaspora caused by the withdrawal of the empire that led them abroad, the effect of metropolitan sentimental "third-worldism" on new nations along with the tyrannical governments and civil wars that have resulted from the withdrawal of imperial order. (83-84)

In a Free State highlights Naipaul's travels through Egypt, Asia, Africa, Europe and America. The stories are set in these places only and speak of the "dangers of freedom" that "exist for most of humankind." The novel appeals existentialist view point though Naipaul like Albert Camus does not attempt "to justify living by the intensity of experience and the fulfillment of pleasure" (King 85). The mingling of genres like travelogues, short stories and a novella demonstrates Naipaul's "conviction that forms have to adapt to meet the fundamental issue of freedom with which he is concerned in the work" (Mohan 98).

The people in these stories and travelogues are in journey in one or the other way; hence familiarize themselves with variety of cultures and beliefs. The journey here provides them to feel the sameness with the other people who are also trying to crave a place for themselves. It becomes a symbol of the world in flux that it portrays. There are people from different continents and countries traveling together in the same ship in the "prologue". On the deck, the variety of races and faces make it easy for Naipaul to forget his own suffering like the Egyptian Greeks are traveling to Egypt which is now "no longer their home but once it used to be" (*In A Free State* 7). They had been expelled from Egypt by invaders. The Egyptian trader and his fellow were "refugee" in their own country which serves as a parallel to Naipaul's experiences. They were brutally humiliated and ousted by the invaders, but after they achieved freedom the poor Egyptians themselves became "the causalities of that freedom" (*In a Free State* 8).

There is one more chapter which presented the metonymy of exile was a "tramp". His very English looks were an attempt to camouflage his original identity. The illusion was broken drastically when he neared to his observer. We saw that all his clothes were in ruin, that the knot on his scarf was tight and grimy; that he was a tramp. When he came to the foot of the gangway, he took off his hat, and we saw that he was "an old man, with a tremulous worn face and wet blue eyes" (*In a Free State* 8). This reality is attempted to be hidden from the world. It is an attempt to hide his powerfulness and his English way of dressing grants him the power enjoyed by the centre.

Naipaul's effort to explore the truth reveals the true identity of the tramp. This old man did not need anything except for a listener as if he wanted to outpour his entire mind to someone interested in his story. His speech was full of dates, places and numbers, with sometimes a simple opinion drawn from another life. But whatever he spoke was delivered in a 'mechanical' manner and was without conviction. As Naipaul estimates:

He wasn't looking for conversation; he didn't even require an audience. The concept of insecurity again is highlighted in his case as he hadn't wanted company; he wanted only the camouflage and protection of company. The tramp knew that he was odd. (*In a Free State* 10)

This oddity has been sensed by Naipaul for himself. This tramp being the most sympathetic of all has been brutally tortured by the Egyptian traders and an Australian boy. He had no escape from that humiliation except for bolting himself inside the cabin and threatening them to set fire to cabin. His distress is emblematic of being caught in a situation where recognition is no more possible without force.

Other two Lebanese on the deck spoke a mixture of French, English and Arabic and Lebanese symbolizes their nomadic lifestyle. Every one of them left their homeland either due to economic reasons or political reasons. Their jealousy with the stable life of native people is an outcome of their diasporic fatigue. For them "nationality" had lost its meaning and significance. One of the tramps says, ". . . but what's nationality these days? I myself, I think if myself as a citizen of the world" (9). This very statement sets a global identity for the displaced and dislocated people for whom national boundary become irrelevant.

They define themselves in the terms of global citizenship. The ship itself was a world in miniature as it was boarded by the people from all over the world. This is the world where the politics of power is seen at its extremes. The tramps for uncertain reasons arouse anger in his fellow companions with whom he shares his cabin and is beaten by them. According to Champa Rao Mohan, "It is made clear that freedom is just an empty word in the imminent chaos that threatens to assert itself and drives people of seek safety in locked cabin" (99).

The novel *In a Free State* comprises three pieces of fiction placed between two pieces of nonfiction, an arrangement that inserts the author into the collection as one of its characters who is themselves exiles and expatriates; its theme is "freedom and loss." The first piece, "Prologue, from a journal: The Tramp at Piraeus," grows out of the instability of Naipaul's life as exile and travel writer and responds dialogically to glorification of the literature. The "Prologue" anticipates the themes to be explored in the three stories that follow it and "Epilogue" concludes the journey leading to no solution. The first story "One Out of Many" is narrated in first person from the point of view of its narrator Santosh. He becomes medium to portray Naipaul's experience of being left in the prison of freedom with responsibility for himself. He is a domestic helper to a Bombay based bureaucrat who migrates to America with his employer when his employer was "seconded by his firm to government service and was posted to Washington as a diplomat" (22). Immediately after his migration Santosh faces the threat of displacement. He remembers his days in Bombay nostalgically. He wishes to revive those bygone days but in vain:

I was so happy in Bombay. I was respected, I had a certain position. I worked for an important man. The highest in the land came to our bachelor chambers and enjoyed my food and showered compliments on me. I also had my friend. We met in the evening on the pavement below the gallery of four chambers. Some of us, like the tailor's bearer and myself, were domestics who lived in the street. (*In a Free State* 21)

Although he belongs to a lower economic class and is illiterate, the discrimination and partial attitude of the plane staff pained him. He was brought to America like a luggage and not like a human being. He feels humiliated and hurt. He is not more than a burden, a luggage for his master who runs the risk of his illegal emigration for his selfish reasons. He had no residential permit or visa or a ticket. Since it was impossible for him to return to his village and to do his "porter's job" he falls into the dilemma to leave the land. At least in Bombay he had an identity though it was as low as a servant. But in America he had to hide himself due to his illegal immigration. Thus, the sense of identity haunts him after leaving India. This sense is intensified further when he meets with a "hubshi" but a free woman. She was a sweeper in his master's building yet she had an independent identity and a home. Now he saw his relationship with his employer in new light. As he remembered his experience and compares the comfort level that he had prior to migration:

My employer had been to me only a presence. I used to tell him that beside him I was as dirt. It was only a way of talking; one of the courtesies of our language, but it had something of truth. I meant that he was the man who adventured in the world for me, that I experienced the world through him, that I was content to be a small part of his presence. (36-37)

But to go to that bygone time and to revive the past is impossible for him. He had to live in America, as a prisoner. The opening of the multiple vistas of a new world brought him new options. He felt happy though initially everything in America gave him a feeling of a stranger trapped in an alien world. He says, "The corridor was long: doors, doors. The illuminated ceiling was decorated with stars of different sizes; the colors were grey and blue and gold. Below that imitation sky I felt like a prisoner" (*In a Free State* 27). He faces the danger of freedom in America. He was afraid when he locked himself out of the apartment:

I hadn't noted the number and didn't even know what floor we were on. My courage flowed out of me. I sat on the floor of the elevator and felt the tears come to my eyes. Almost without noise the elevator door closed, and I found I was being taken up silently at great speed. (27)

Despite, he enjoys his newly found freedom for a few days but realizes very soon that freedom brings responsibility which he must face alone. Unable to bear the burden of his freedom, Santosh is on the verge of breaking down and leans back to his previous psychological state of dependence. His relationship with Priya undergoes a change, when instead of calling Priya by her name as he had done from the beginning, in the stupor of his fear; he suddenly addresses Priya as "Sahib", thus, reaffirming the master slave relationship. Santosh immediately realizes his mistake:

I had used the wrong word. Once I had used the word a hundred times a day. But then I had considered myself a small part of my employer's presence, and the word was not servile; it was mere like a name, like a reassuring sound, part of my employer's dignity and therefore part of mine.

But Priya's dignity could never be mine; that was not out relationship. (48)

At the end, Santosh discloses everything to his new friend and also tells about his fear of being thrown away in lack of a citizenship. On Priya's advice he marries a "*hubshi*" woman and becomes a legal citizen of America. But he realizes that the freedom for a displaced person can be nothing more than imprisonment as he suffered the alienation and fragmentation throughout his life. Santosh feels that the restaurant is one world, the parks and green streets of Washington are another, and every evening some of these streets take me to a third. Since the beginning of his journey, he was trying to break the shackles of slavery. His urge to "become a free man" leads him to a different state of freedom but it also brings the disappointment, as he feels, "All that my freedom has brought me is the knowledge that I have a face and have a body, that I must feed this body and clothe this body for a certain number of years. Then it will be over" (58).

As a dislocated person Santosh is obsessed with a sense of locating his world and identity in an alien world. The next story "Tell Me Who to Kill" takes us to the West Indies. The narrator is from a distant village. He suffered more than the previous protagonist and the cause of his suffering is his younger brother, who is caught in the glitter of the Western World. He loses everything including his sense of identity in Europe while searching for his brother. Again, the return is impossible for him like Santosh as these characters live in on the edge of existence. Having been denied an opportunity to make a mark in life, he nurtures the dreams of a better life for his brother Dayo. He becomes the focus of his life. His self-effacement is so intense that he remains Dayo's brother till end and has no name in the story. His identity takes a backseat.

The narrator in this story belongs to lower economic strata and has illiterate parents. His uncle and aunt comparatively literate live in the town. His job of a cart driver can afford him a meager earning only sufficient for his bread and butter. He speaks of the responsibility on his shoulders that he has to cater as the head of the family in the absence of his father:

I feel I become like the head of the family. I get the ambition and the same for all of them. The ambition is like shame, and same is like a secret, and it is always hurting. Even now, when it is all over, it can start hurting again. (65)

He sacrificed his life to make his brother's dreams come true. As the theme goes, he also gets disillusioned in the last for his commitments. The story also reveals certain myths of Caribbean multi-racial society. The people like his uncle Stephen think Christianity as a symbol of "progressive". People convert themselves or they adopt false identity to show themselves strong and prestigious. He tells Frank in England about his uncle:

My father's brother is living in the city. How he gets there, how he get education when my father gets none, how he gets this job with the lawyer, all of this happen a long time ago, before I was born, and is now like a mystery. He is a Christian, or he take a Christian name, Stephen, as a mark of his progressiveness, but all of us enjoy the little fame and respect he gives us in the village. (68)

The illusion which he had regarding his uncle in his Caribbean life was broken completely when he visited his uncle in the city and discovered the dwarfish lifestyle they lived. He felt that they were living like "seven dwarfs, with their little foreign pictures in their drawing- room." His uncle, Stephen feels proud on sending his son abroad for studies. So, he, too, wanted to send his brother according to his wish to study "Aeronautical Engineering". He is fascinated by the terms he used and the accent his brother was learning from the city life. He manages to send him there, and later he also goes to London to take care of him. This journey proves to be an eye opener for him as it disillusions him and breaks all the myths regarding empire and its urban lifestyle.

Dayo represents the people who arrive in London seeking a better future, but become victims. In London, life is not as easy as it appears for them. Dayo tells his brother; it is not easy to take studies in this place as you and other people believe. Dayo becomes the subject of the sympathy of the readers when he becomes aimless as he could not live up to the expectations of his brother. He was initially ridiculed by his aunt and his cousins for his poverty and slow wit. His cousin, Stephen's son also reaches to the same destiny in London. Both of them belonging to same island and ancestry face the similar consequences in an "alien land". It proves fatal consequence of expatriation and the freedom granted by immigration leads them into imperishable troubles.

The narrator of the story suffers a nervous breakdown when Dayo marries an English girl. His hatred for his uncle's love of Christianity and English culture is again revived by the act of his own brother. He blames it on the people in London. He cries in anguish:

I love them. They take my money, they spoil my life, and they separate us. But they can't kill them. O God, show me the enemy. Once you find out who the enemy is, you can kill him. But these people here they confuse me. Who hurt me? Who spoils my life? Tell me who to beat back. Tell me who to kill. (102)

Actually, the story of "Tell Me Who to Kill" can be read as a story of exile and of the continuing effects of colonialism on people of developing societies. At the story's conclusion the narrator unable to ascertain the reason for his failure, he can only vent his pain and bewilderment.

Thus, the enemy of a native is an alien land remains invisible and frustration is diverted towards the self. There is a feeling of separation in him regarding his brother and uncle who preferred West more than their own country. Dayo's marriage to an alien girl breaks their links forever. He reminisces nostalgically his childhood lived in a secluded island where his brother was entirely dependent on him, and shared an unbearable bond with him. It is beyond his power to face the reality in London. He ultimately feels that his life had been ruled by his decision to move to England. His state of agony is a typical outcome of his alienation which he experiences in London in lack of his brother. Champa Rao Mohan remarks:

Disillusionment with England forms the major theme of "Tell Me Who to Tell." Freedom becomes a state of being aimless and adrift, a severance of all ties with the world—a total withdrawal. The narrator, who cannot bear to return home after his failure, sends back a message that he is dead. He has been reduced to a living corpse. (104)

The novella "In a Free State" throws light upon Africa in political turmoil side by side, which has got its independence recently. It portrays the earliest settlers with compassion, showing their toughness, brutality, illusion and hopes to create a better European life abroad and willingness to stay on when times get tough. Bruce King opines about the role of these English men in Africa:

They built for the future whereas the new class of postcolonial experts, advisors and liberal sympathizers are parasites, with no genuine commitment. They are on short-contracts and will move on when they can, whereas the older colonialists have become too old to start again. (86)

The sensitive narrative of the story reflects the rift between the colonized and the colonizer. The enmity between the black and the white occupies the centre of the narrative. It is set in Africa undergoing an upheaval. The story comes through the consciousness of Bobby, who is a white administrative officer in one of the departments of central government and lives in the Southern Collectorate, a territory of the King's people. The opening of the story depicts that Bobby is in the capital, "a four-hundred-mile drive from the collectorate", attending a seminar on "community development."

In Africa tribes there are people who prefer "presidential rule" and are fighting their soul out for their will. The territories are divided and authoritarians are yielding its major states. The opening lines vividly express the condition and prevalent tension among the people:

In this country in Africa there was a president and there was also a king. They belonged to different tribes. The enmity of the tribes was old, and with independence their anxieties about one another became acute. The king and the president intrigued with the local representatives of white governments. The white men who were appealed to like the king personally. But the president was stronger; the new army was wholly his, of his tribe; and the white men decided that the president was to be supported. So that at last, this weekend, the president was able to send his army against the king's people. (103)

In such tense condition there are a few white people who are left in Africa and are still working in an English-Indian atmosphere of Africa wilderness. It was still a colonial city with a colonial glamour. Everyone in it was "for from home". It is a typical colonial country where many races reside and "racial incidents" are a commonplace. Mimicry is the common metaphor of life which is visible in the behavior and daily routine of the native Africans. Bobby observes in the country bar that "they drank shorter, prettier drinks with cocktail sticks and wore English-made suit" (104). They adopt a typical English hairstyle. This mimicry grants them imaginary freedom that transforms them into "the men of power". In the new Africa, they were "high civil servants, directors, and managing directors of recently opened branches of big international corporations" (104).

Bobby, the narrator is a white man, who faces atrocious conditions and brutal treatment of the natives in the capital Shropshire and in other places just because of his white skin color. Naipaul is nowhere seen sympathetic for those white diaspora people. In Naipaul's other stories, it is the black or the colonized that are caught in an alien land alone. They suffer due to their status of minority in empirical land. It is a fine contrast with his other stories as it deals with a "white" powerless person cast into a dark land. Bobby and other people, who belonged to the majority in their country and empowered during colonization are victimized one by one in the "dark country". Bobby left England due to the nervous "breakdown" in London due to his commonness among his own people. Africa "saved" his life as it provided him the authority and distinction and a racial superiority. In London he as well his friend Martin both felt lost among similar people and comparatively powerful competitors of the same race.

In a Free State is very much like Conrad's *Heart of Darkness*. The novel is a record of a journey through bush and forest between Outposts of European civilization in Africa. Bobby, an English administrative officer in a former British colony, derives by car from the nation's capital to a government compound up-country; Linda, an acquaintance and the wife of a British official who also loves at the compound, travel with him. Upon her urging, they stop along the way at a hunting lodge run by a crusty former British colonel with whom Linda apparently spends the night. The next day they continue their journey but encounter rain and bad roads and are unable to reach the Southern Collectorate before the four o'clock. Curfew is in effect because a secessionist movement threatens the national government. Driving through the region of the rival, secessionist tribe, Bobby and Linda pass menacing army Lorries, the abandoned vehicle of the tribe's king, who has been killed, and a line of his supporters now held as prisoners by government soldiers.

Bobby seems to have realized his place, as he informed Linda that he was there "to serve" and not to "tell them how to run their country" (118). His tone reflects his pain yet he tries his best to sound neutral. He indirectly clarifies their marginal condition in Africa. It is made evident that president's victory in the ongoing civil war could cause more troubles for them. His views are quite imperial in tone as he thinks like missionaries. According to him African must get food and school and hospitals regardless of its government. Bobby adopts a liberal attitude and tries to sort out the reasons behind the problems of whites in Africa. It is their attitude in the times of imperial collapse which is responsible for their insecurities and humiliation.

He shows his amazement for the whites in Africa who think that "Africans don't have eyes" (118). Now as he feels that the time has come, they should leave it to the natives, he stops discussing it with passion.

Linda finds Masai women attractive, tall and elegant and Bobby finds black color fascinating. They both express a wish to be born as the natives of Africa, as their white color poses threats to their existence. Their wishes portray their desires to hold on to the power. Africa, a place where people from all the continents have settled, is frankly considered as a world colony. This is a place where hatred, disgust and racial rifts are a daily affair. Bobby tells Linda about the situation of the capital, as the "Traffic to the capital was light but steady: old lorries, tankers driven by turbaned Sikhs, a few European and Asian cars, African driven Peugeot estate-car, often looking brand-new, always speeding with rocking African" (120).

People are divided into sects and vary in opinions, like English want king's rule that will maintain their authority, whereas Asians prefer democracy and president rule, whereas, Africans are confused between the two. For Linda it is unusual to see white men working under natives as Bobby does under Ogguna Wanga- Butere. Africa needs white people but racial hatred overpowers their importance:

Every day the president travels up and down, telling his people that we are needed. But he is no fool. He knows the old colonial hands are out to get every penny they can before they scuttle south. We lecture the Africans about corruption. But there is a lot of anguish and talk about prejudice when they rumble our little rackets. (124)

While Bobby and Linda traveled all along on an African landscape, Naipaul presents a shocking example of Natives causing trouble to white men. Bobby's stay in independent Africa is a reverse expatriation. White people are victimized in Africa as they challenge African symmetry. They have been colonials thus symbolize power but independent Africa refuses their stay. They have to face humiliation and disgust in exile as Blacks have suffered in Europe. The symmetries have been inverted as the equations of diasporic binaries remain same.

At a "Hunting Lodge" on the way they meet African people serving as servants. They are informed by Carter, a white fellow at lodge that the "expatriate" places including the Collectorate were in curfew due to the increasing tension between tribes. He is advised to stay safe and not to go to the Collectorate office. Yet Bobby decides to drive back to Collectorate. As he drove back his car, an African woman in rags stopped them to get a lift for her son. The boy filled the car with his 'filthy smell' and made it suffocation for Linda. Bobby's liberal and friendly attitude gave way to the indecent behavior of the boy, who asked him first to stop to take a "completely soaked" native in and later to drop them at a destination, which was surely not falling in Bobby's direction. Naipaul in this episode indicates at the power shift. Africans now do not feel subjugated instead they are turning the table on the colonials, and are avenging them. Though the war is between the tribes, and the whites are considered "neutral", they have fair chances of being harassed. Linda and Bobby are harassed for they remind them of their colonial masters.

From the sense and incident, it is clear that there is racial bond between Bobby and Linda which brings them closer despite his remaining aloof from her and their opposite opinions. The picture that emerges about the state of affairs in this country is that of the total chaos. The educated Africans, who are the new men of Africa, turn out to be "the mimic men". As Champa Rao Mohan points out that "they remain as inarticulate as their brothers in the bush villages" (105). Everything in Africa is under suspicion. The situation that prevails in Africa is conveyed through the image of the hunting dogs that have gone wild on being abandoned by their masters. These dogs have been habitual of their masters to attack the natives. They have posed a threat to almost everyone sparing none.

His long drive enables him to revive his attitude towards the Africans and correct his misconceptions about Africa. Bobby undoubtedly thanks Africa for his survival but he is interested into these affairs merely for his own sake. Though he has an "over-friendly" patronizing attitude to the blacks, he cannot help himself feeling superior to them. It is clear that Bobby knows where he stands after the equations of power have been inverted. When the President's soldiers beat him up, there is little he can do besides nursing his wounds, both physical and psychological. When Bobby gets back to the compound, Luke, his house boy laughs at him. The story concludes with Bobby realizing that he would have to leave eventually, but first he would have to dismiss Luke before whom he has been exposed. Finally, it was the power and authority which brought him here and now it is the same thing that may carry him back. Here Bruce King's words seem in place:

> Freedom not only creates crises of purpose and responsibility but also brings dangers of insecurity and ruin. Freedom from moral right and wrong also has its dangers as Bobby learns in attempting to seduce African men. Freedom from established manners produces such

absurdities as Santosh's purchase of a green suit. (*In a Free State* 88)

A free or independent state can be a chaotic, disordered and violent nation in the midst of a civil war. Freedom can result in tyranny. The various pieces of narration in the text exemplify the similar state. Naipaul has created the characters after "the stereotyped and dehumanized version propagated by the colonizers" (Mohan 108).

In *In a Free State*, Naipaul has especially highlighted the violence of post-independence Africa. Ania Loomba points out that the internal fracture or fissures existed alongside colonialism surfaces after independence in the countries in Africa and Asia. With the European colonial expanded, and nation-building, the violence and aggression were intensified, expanded and reworked. She remarks:

Thus laziness, aggression, violence, greed, sexual promiscuity, bestiality, innocence and irrationality are attributed (often contradictorily and inconsistently) by the English, French, Dutch, Spanish and Portuguese colonists to Turks, Africans, Native American, Jews, Indians, the Irish, and others. (107)

The above stated themes, to some extent, categorize Naipaul's work. In *In A Free State* the violence and sexual interferences and native aggression are a few traits of fractured identity of African natives, which come to the fore. Bobby faces the anger of a Zulu in the public bar, and remains silent because he understands his position in an intensely violent place. Contact with racially 'others' in Africa is structured by the imperatives of racial differences.

Naipaul presents one more colonial problem of presenting the local population in a prejudiced way, which has a profound impact on racial discourses and identities. The concluding part of *In a Free State* is an epilogue from a journal, entitled "The Circus at Luxor". Naipaul again like the prologue gives an account of his journey to Egypt, but this time by air. If he was quite detached with incidents in the "prologue", then in "epilogue" he makes an unexpected gesture of involvement. He breaks his journey in Milan in a bad weather so he had to leave it in snow along with the circus on Chinese people. In the epilogue he physically intervenes to put a stop to the drama of human misery and indignity he witnesses in Luxor. At an oasis "rest-house" in Cairo he witnesses the extreme poverty as the children starved. They picked the scraps of food which were thrown on the sand by the tourists. They get whips from the coffee-waiter as they neared the tourist place. He points out the oddity of the place:

A brisk middle-aged Egyptian in Arab dress moved among the tables and served coffee. He had a camel-whip at his waist, and I saw, but only slowly, that for some way around the rest-horse the hum-mocked sand was alive with little desert children. The desert was clean, the air was clean; these children were very dirty. (*In a Free State* 241)

The only medium for Naipaul to associate with the crowed is European language as he communicates with two Germans who could understand him. But the sensitivity of these Germans was not as sharp as his so they overlooked the children being beaten up on the deck. He could not bear the torture on the little children. He rushes to the scene and puts a stop to the act by snatching the whip from the waiter. He writes:

Still the Germans at my table didn't notice; the students inside were still talking. I saw that my hand was trembling. I put down the sandwich I was eating on the metal table; it was my last decision. Lucidity and anxiety came to me only when I was almost on the man with the camel-whip. I was shouting. I took the whip away, threw it on the sand. (243)

Though he felt relieved by the action as he couldn't control himself, yet he associates his attitude with inferiority. He felt exposed, futile and he wanted to get back to his table. But now it was a little different as he found himself in a free state and he did not have to look for the approval for his behavior. In Luxor, Naipaul tries to survey the landscape for a historical context by linking the present-day landscape of Egypt to the past. When he sees the ancient ruins, he in his mind tries to get a sense of the past by isolating it from the present distress of Egypt. The landscape represented in the paintings by ancient artists portrayed a well-ordered place and the people having a sense of place.

Having traveled almost all the continents, Naipaul feels dissatisfied with portrayal of a perfect world in the pictures. He guesses, "Perhaps that had been the only pure time, at the beginning, when the ancient artist, knowing no other land, had learned to look at his own and had seen it as complete" (246).

Naipaul's conclusion is based on ultimate truths of all postcolonial societies as the conditions of one colony are similar to the other colonies in a particular way. Naipaul has been successful in his attempt to highlight the effects of colonialism on the culture and psyche of the colonized people.

In this way these accounts are fairly nostalgic in tone. He talks of various incidents, situations and experiences in fragments by mingling fantasy with reality, the environment and the geographical conditions of his native land in a descriptive manner. He reflects his feelings and emotions through his characters. History plays a vital role in these writings. In these texts history is linked with reality as it also emphasizes a particular period of his personal life or events pertaining to history. Being real and appropriate they are read and accepted as the real and authentic accounts:

The text is a tissue of meaning, perceptions and responses which inhere in the first place in that imaginary production of the real which is ideology. The "textual real" is related to the historical real. Not as an imaginary transposition of it, but as the product of certain signifying practices whose source and referent are, in the last instance, history itself. (Mishra 29)

Language in these texts has been used as major tool to express nostalgia. Language is the most effective medium to communicate with each other among human beings; and if the language fails then the individual feels handicapped. Living in an alien land an individual cannot speak his native language. He is unable to communicate with the fellow people. Diasporic writers use their native language in their writings. The characters speak in their mother tongue. There may be a frequent use of words, through which one comes to know to which nation an individual belongs to. These texts express Naipaul's diasporic stature variously giving a vivid account of his autobiographical and universal predicament of being cast into an alien world.

A Bend in the River displays an acute awareness of transitional complexities of belonging and identity entailed in the diasporic experience. It turns the reader's attention to the underprivileged diasporic being, and those who find themselves in the midst of a global space to which they cannot relate. It is not the attachment to home that concerns the diasporic characters in the novel, but rather the dramatic loss of home and the desire to be at home. Naipaul highlights the state of subaltern being neither-here-nor-there of peoples of the diaspora, who trouble the idea of citizenship and national belonging on the one hand and represent the new force of cosmopolitans on the other hand. In *A Bend in the River*, diaspora and cosmopolitanism appear closely related as ways of understanding transnational identities. Diasporic and cosmopolitan lifestyles constitute overlapping repertoires that offer complementary identifications for immigrants, especially those with prior experiences of (post) colonial contact zones, in diverse cultural settings.

In the novel having African setting, Naipaul is in the grip of a complex vision which enables him to portray the ambivalence among the denizens of those unfortunate countries that have just toppled out of a tribal past, or freed themselves from colonial rule but cannot reach the uncertain blessings of modernity. He is obsessed with the hollowness of these proclaimed liberations. Thus, Africa provides Naipaul with a setting within which he can further ascertain and develop his propositions about the collapse of the Third World. Its setting provides Naipaul with what happens to be another testing ground for his theories. The dilemma of belongingness itself converts an expatriate into a state of subaltern when Salim says:

Africa was my home, had been the home of my family for centuries. But we came from the east coast, and that made the difference. The coast was not truly African. It was an Arab-Indian-Persian-Portuguese place, and we who lived there were really people of the Indian Ocean. True Africa was at our back. Many miles of scrub or desert separated us from the up-country people; we looked east to the lands, with which we traded— Arabia, India, Persia. These were also the lands of our ancestors. (*A Bend in the River* 10-11)

According to Bruce King, the novel *A Bend in the River* covers a decade roughly from 1965 to 1975. The novel is based on Naipaul's observation of Zaire and East Africa. Many incidents in the novel are suggested by previous writing about Africa, especially what Naipaul has termed the literature on Imperialism where Africa is a backdrop for the crisis of some European or African character. The novel is set in a newly independent Francophone central African state governed by dictatorial former Army officer Big Man.

In this state Big Man has restored the peace and law and order, as he carries an impressive staff representing power of an African chief. Big Man sold a "little Maoist green book" to the general population of Africa and transformed its youth in a "national youth brigade" which marches while shouting slogans. To put in Bruce King's words "colonial mimicry of Europe" in Africa now "includes mimicry of Maoist China" (118).

Moreover, Salim from a rootless diasporic community without any impressive educational background, is twice displaced and transplanted in Africa, as he voluntarily escapes from his home and community to live in another African country. In this sense, he epitomizes absolute rootlessness. Then, the main issue about rootless people like Salim who voluntarily cut off their already diasporic racial and social ties seems initially to be that of detachment or involvement, passivity or action, flight or integration. Is the ideal detachment or rootlessness that the old cosmopolitanism advocates psychologically and socially viable? Is there equilibrium between detachment and attachment, rootlessness and rootedness?

Salim introduces himself as an exile and stranger in a state of detachment and insecurity in his own family and community. He says:

So, from an early age I developed the habit of looking, detaching myself from a familiar scene and trying to consider it as from a distance. It was from this habit of looking that the idea came to me that as a community we had fallen behind. And that was the beginning of my insecurity (17).

He recognizes the un-protectedness and weakness of the Indian diaspora in Africa in the face of the struggle for power following the withdrawal of the colonial order. He explains his insecurity about the fatalism of his decaying and static community as his temperament. In fact, his lack of religious consciousness is largely responsible:

My own pessimism and my insecurity were a more terrestrial affair. I was without the religious sense of my family. The insecurity I felt was due to my lack of true religion, and was like the small change of the exalted pessimism of our faith, the pessimism that can drive men on to do wonders. (18)

In most of Naipaul's novels the central characters are exposed to colonial power and are left with no protection against the imperial forces. Their lives undergo the rapid changes and consequently become easy victims of the instable postcolonial condition. Salim, an East Indian trader in central part of Africa does not know about Ferdinand's (his little Negro assistant) intention, yet he observes the changes in this little black boy.

Although Naipaul does not attempt to create black African characters in depth, Salim says he does not know what is going on in the mind of Ferdinand and has no acquaintance with village life – "the Africa of corruption, a new insecure bourgeois, tribal conflict, food shortages and tyrannical government is present" (King 118). Here Naipaul draws closer to the classic writers of Africa such as Achebe and Wole Soyinka who have portrayed an impressive picture of Africa form an indigenous point of view, yet his commitment to Africa of not so intense as of those who long for pure African writings. His deepest sympathies are with the Indian threatened by African nationalism and political disorder. But such disorder is found to be universal, partly the result of the withdrawal of the older imperial order, partly a continuing process throughout history. Salim is alienated by the racial differences and therefore he is harassed by the natives several times due to his Indian-Arabian lineage. He feels helpless about the teen Africans despite knowing them as the rebellious youth. He thus becomes a self-alienated particularity in his own community. Salim not only refuses to associate himself with but also feels disappointed at his community's shared tastes and values.

Salim decides that breaking out of his social and racial ties and being rootless is the only way out. He explains:

I had to break away from our family compound and our community. To stay with my community, to pretend that I had simply to travel along with them, was to be taken with them to destruction. I could be master of my fate only if I stood alone. (*A Bend in the River* 22)

The "wonder" that Salim does, driven by his pessimism, is to take over a shop that Nazruddin offers him in a far-off African country. He chooses to cross from the east coast right through to the centre of the continent, and to start his new life there alone. Salim's boundary-crossing journey at the opening of the novel is an indication that his identity will be a constant in-betweenness in perpetual becoming through his negotiation with different spaces.

Bruce King calls *A Bend in the River* the big bang novel as Naipaul focuses on the postcolonial situation in Africa here. It deals with the civil war of Africa, power shift, and role reversal between whites and blacks and the theme of homosexuality in the troubled times of Africa. The protagonist of the text feels like an outcast thus it also has the shreds of diasporic literature. Salim has Indian lineage but equally feels attached with Africa as he considers it his "home". His family had been living here for centuries with a difference that they came from east coast which was not truly African. Rather it was Arab-Indian-Persian-Portuguese place, and his family was Muslims. Salim says, "We were a special group. We were distinct from the Arabs and other Muslims of the coast; in our customs and attitudes we were closer at the Hindus of North-Western India, from which we had originally come" (*A Bend In the River* 17).

Salim belongs to Africa and has nowhere to go, yet he feels detached to African culture due to his racial and Indian links. Talking about his ancestral link with India and Africa, he understands his grandfather's inability to relate himself with the dates of past. For him past was simply the past. Apart from this, whatever else he knew; it was through the book written by Europeans without which he thinks "all our past would have been washed away" (18). He also traces the history of two slave families living in his family's compound. But now the present was all changed and they were now merely servants. The idea of Africa as a country came through British administration. Salim due to his strange relationship had to adopt certain strategies to survive painlessly. He says:

So, from an early age I developed the habit of looking, detaching myself from a familiar scene and trying to consider it as from a distance. It was from this habit of looking that the idea came to me that as a community we had fallen behind. And that was the beginning of my security. (*A Bend in the River* 22)

In Naipaul, the feeling of insecurity is to a great extent, affiliated to imperialism and colonial invasions. Salim too feels insecure due to his racial difference which was an outcome of his grandfather's immigration. This insecurity came to a sharp surge by decolonization and African tribal wars. It is looked at as a weakness and a failing of his own temperament.

He felt exposed and helpless if his migrant status is revealed in any conversation. He compares his ancestors and Arabs who once conquered and ruled Africa before Europeans. He finds that his people had fallen prey to the changes occurred to the land and were feeling vulnerable to the rising tribal powers. There is a racial disparity which he opines, resulted in white supremacy of the Europeans who could assess themselves. Salim finds that the European were better equipped to cope with changes than we were. He also says:

When I compared the European with us that we had ceased to count in Africa, then really, we no longer had anything to offer. The Europeans were preparing to get out, or to fight, to meet the Africans half-way. We continued to live as we had always done, blindly. (23)

In the above passage Salim echoes Naipaul's opinion about Islam, as stated variously in his two books dealing with Islam, *Beyond Belief* and *Among the Believers*. Naipaul condemns Islam as "catastrophic, a belief-system that, like colonialism, attempt to enslave or destroy other cultures" (Mittapalli 69). Salim too feels that it is the restrictedness of Islamic culture that made them shrink in a part of Africa.

Salim's family was of traders, businessmen, who could "assess the situation" and sometime took very bold risks.

When things went wrong there was always a consolation of religion. It was the time African unrest in North, which even British felt unable to put down. Due to bloody rebellion, it was the time for departure for mixed race population. As the nationalists and youth brigade of Big Man getting powerful, natives had stood as a big threat for Hindus and Muslims. Inder, Salim's rich friend says, "We're washed up here you know. To be in Africa you have to be strong. We're not strong. We don't even have a flag" (24).

Salim's decision to stay back in the heart of Africa, despite his sense of insecurity and inability to protect anyone makes him the subject of ridicule for Inder. He decided to "break away" from his family and become the master of his own fate which was possible only if he stood alone. For Salim it was a little difficult to be firm on his decision to live alone as African coasts were trying to save themselves from racial disparity and bloody tribal rebellion.

Nazruddin, an elderly man of Salim's community, was known for his European manners and did his Arab business "in the centre of the continent, at the bend in the river" (26). In Salim's words he was an exotic as he kept on selling his property at one place and buying at another. Uganda is a new destination for him which can fetch gold to him. He advised Salim, yet not offered anything openly, to move to Uganda as it was more peaceful where native struggle was not there. Salim chooses to be a businessman in one of his old shops in the centre of Africa at the bend in the river against the wishes of his family and the friends.

The town that Salim finds over there was populated by Belgians, Greeks, Italians, Arabs, and Africans. The grandeur of the city explained by Nazruddin was fairly the part of the relics, it was like the site of a dead civilization as the sun and rain and bush had made the site like old. Though Africa has been ruined and as now a vainglorious thing, yet there are people like Father Huismans who don't think themselves as the part of the "bush", instead they feel the immense flow of history in Africa. They consider themselves as the part of that history. Everyone in Africa was living with his own idea of the place and civilization. For Salim it was the bush devoid of culture; for the Father, it was the part of Europe and it was difficult to delineate from its European colonial impact.

He felt insecure because he stressed his Europeanness, therefore holding the imperial hangover in the centre. His love of Africa gives space to Conradian spirit of adventure. For Father Huismans colonial relics were as precious as the tings of Africa. He saw true Africa as dying or about to die. He consumed himself with the love of collecting pieces of dying Africa, yet he had immense love for the things which were related to Europe. His desperation to be affiliated with the stepping of European colonial power and "stupendous idea of the future" made him see himself as "the last, lucky witness" (70).

The "river" which signifies the "flow of culture and civilization" has always been the place of settlement for outsiders. John Cooke, as quoted in Serafin Roldan Santiago's article "V. S. Naipaul's *A Bend in The River:* Caricature as social and Political Criticism", observes that, "a river's flow represents the passage of time; the hyacinth-choked river is an image of cultural stagnation. The vein attempts of the villagers to remove the hyacinths show the futility of trying to bring this town into history" (Mittapalli 142).

The city has been completely turned into ruins due to the "depth of that African rage, the wish to destroy, regardless of the consequences". Now there was nothing like a social life. "The expatriate wasn't welcoming". For a trader like Salim, it was quite difficult to survive and unwise to stay there. Everywhere there were relics of "colonial days." In these devastating circumstances of the city, people were feeling uncertain about everything as their social milieu was dwindling day by day. Power shift was another cause of fear among them. The oppressed people had adopted the role of oppressors. Now Metty alias Ali no more liked to be called Salim's servant; instead, he preferred to be an independent like Ferdinand. Salim feels a little shocked by the changing behavior of these African lads as they ceased to hesitate from asking for the favor from him despite having evil intention for him.

Metty after adopting the free atmosphere of the city started redefining his relationship with Salim. Now he called him his "patron" instead master. Salim allowed it to happen as there was nothing, he could do to prevent him "doing indecent things" such as dancing, and coming late in the night. Salim took it in another way. Metty had a free talk with every native that helped him to enhance his business. Along with it he also helped him.

Racial differences become more acute when sergeant Iyanda was killed openly by white soldiers in the rebellion. Sergeant Iyanda belonged to the socially abominable slave tribe of Africa and therefore was disliked by the local people. Here Naipaul brings the slim line of distinction among the Africans which heightens the racial difference among the Blacks and defies Negro unity. As an impact of imperialism whites are preferably respected and followed by the locals. They imitate their "master" which speaks of colonial hegemony as a sign of progress. Salim understands the reason of the subsequent zeal and enthusiasm among the African over the matter. He wonders about "the news of his execution would have pleased the local people. Not that he was a wicked man; but he belonged to that detested slave-hunting tribe, the rest of his army, like his colonial" (*A Bend in The River* 82).

Tabish Khair finds this as an indication of the Africans being childish or "immature" as they are "irrational" and are doing "mimicry" in the lack of "history". There is a semblance of alienation in Salim due to persistent "cultural conflict" in his mind. His views about Africa were quite different from that of a common African or a professional business man. He thought that "there was treasure around us, waiting to be picked. It was the bush that gave us this feeling (102). For the first time he started sharing the boom and peace of Africa. Though he considerably feels himself separated from an average man as in his "own mind I separated myself form them". He still thought of himself as a man just passing through. He is completely clueless about the future unlike Nazruddin. In his separate world he was surrounded by his own "anxieties and became almost dissatisfied and restless" which was an outcome of outside pressure as well as his "solitude" which has become his permanent temperament.

Under the terror Salim feels that the "free-for-all of independence had come to an end" as the legally unrecognized army was sent by the president himself to slay the innocent population of the area. He was igniting and participating in the inter-racial and tribal was himself due to his personal prejudices. He wanted to create another Europe in Africa in the form of "New Doman". There is a sharp contradiction between the traditional Africa and the modern vision of the Big Man:

The Bend was written in Wiltshire where Naipaul was among the ancient Druid and Roman ruins of England contributed to his feeling of history as consisting of repeated cycles of the rise of cultures and empires which will end in decay. One of the themes of the novel is the contradiction between wanting a traditional culture rooted in the village life of the past and wanting a modern Europeanized state, European technology and comforts. This conflict, which is inherent to most nationalist movements, is a theme of Naipaul's writings. (King 126)

Colonial system has made the mindsets of the African people rigid and fixed some or the other ways. The Big Man has modulated New Domain in an imitation of Europe and America. Yevette, the wife of white historian Raymond, who is very close to the president, express her view on the colonial dress code popular in Africa in postcolonial times, "I wish he would change boy's uniform, the good old colonial style of short trousers and a jacket, but not the carnival costume of short trousers and jacket" (*A Bend in The River* 140).

At the centre of the novel is Salim, a Muslim of an Indian family which has lived for several generations in a coastal town, trading quietly, and pitted in traditionalism. He identifies his family as Muslim, but as "a special group distinct from the Arabs and other Muslims of the coast; in our customs and attitudes we were closer to the Hindus of North-Western India, which we had originally come" (*A Bend in the River* 17).

Both from the narrative voice and dominant consciousness, Salim is a decent impressionable, thoughtful, but not at all intellectual. He is an outsider, watching with the outsider's nervousness. Salim's escape from small, restricted society for a new life in Central

Africa is hardly rewarding as it is more suffocating and endangered than the life he has fled. In the new environment, his only contacts are with a few other aliens and expatriates. He develops an intimate relationship with an Indian couple—Mahesh and Shoba who live enclosed self-centered lives of their own, cut off from the African world which surrounds them. This couple has escaped the foes of inter-caste love match, fearing family relation. Now they live only for themselves, obsessed as they are with the romance of their extraordinary union in a world preoccupied with the idea of racial discrimination and casteism. For them, the idea of nation and national identity has lost the meaning. A nation, according to Ernest Renan:

Is a soul, a spiritual principle one lies in the past, one in the present. One is the possession in common of a rich legacy of memories; the other is present day consent, the desire to live together, the will to perpetuate the value of the heritage that one has received in an undivided form. The wish of nations is, all in all, the sole legitimate criterion, the one to which one must always return. (19-20)

Big man's policy of radicalization of business belonging to foreigners destroys property rights and introduces a further disorder and injustice beyond the simple corruption and violence depicted earlier in the novel. This is conscious corruption and perversion of truth and order. African are given business they do not own and the owners become managers and everyone becomes hysterical to amass wealth before the imminent chaos as the country slides quickly towards another rebellion. After his business is given to Theotime, for whom he now works, Salim increasingly becomes aware that he is defenseless and an easy prey for others. As he needs to save money to escape, Salim stops being able to help Metty:

I could no longer offer him the simple protection he had asked for Theotime made that plain during the course of the day. So the old contract between Metty and myself, which was the contract between his family and mine came to an end our special contract was over. He seemed to understand this, and it made him unbalanced. (*A Bend in the River* 273-74)

By the end, the Big Man has radicalized the country and assigned Salim's little shop to Citizen Theotine, who, according to Salim, wants himself to be acknowledged as the boss. Arrested and thrown into jail, Salim is finally saved by the town's new commissioner, Ferdinand, only yesterday a stumbling boy from the village.

Raymond feels a little insecure about the statement and assures that it is surely not the same colonial replica of army dress but everybody in uniform has to feel that he has a personal contact with the president. It is a matter of fact that in the countries like Africa where pre-colonial civilization was either tribal or in primitive state, it is almost impossible to eliminate the sense of mimicry as now in post-colonial times it has assumed a form of identity. Yet Raymond finds a very obvious dichotomy among them.

They may be adopting and accepting colonial manners and dress codes but they wouldn't agree to be ruled by a colonial ruler. They need an African to rule Africa, "which the colonial did not understand and had to leave the land" (141). The Africans now identify themselves with the president in new Domain. The portrait of the president is considered as the portrait of the "self" by a common African. The outsiders will in any case be treated as the outsiders.

The novel explores the adverse times of the continent when political turmoil is a thing of only concern. Whites feel insecure, Indian migrant people feel tortured and African see themselves as the new race going to dominate the entire landscape. There also lurks the theme of homosexuality, as it gives a hint that Africans are no more left in the dark world, they have adopted all those things which are the sign of western culture or "progressive deformity".

In the above-mentioned novels this is evident that Naipaul has minutely studied all the societies he has traveled through. Because of cultural and racial differences, he finds a common constituent forming almost all global societies in postcolonial era. Each of the novels refers to entirely different communities yet they have a strikingly similar social construction due to their colonial past. They have suffered the historical setbacks recently and in remote past, subjugation, domination, expatriation and displacement are a common destiny of the people in these countries. There have been jubilant efforts to prove their intellectual potential and attempts to write back to the empire by these third world societies recently.

The people being distinctly aware of class struggle clash with each other to achieve prominence in the social hierarchy in the post-colonial societies of Africa and Caribbean. Thus, it would be logical to conclude that these novels have profound foregrounding in class struggle and put the subaltern in the margin in a socially and culturally fragmented society.

The principal characters in *A Bend in the River* are aliens. They are Asians, European settlers or expatriates, members of different tribes/ ethnic groups, or people of a mixed ancestry that denies them authentic status. This displacement has always been one of Naipaul's themes and, for him; it serves as a device that allows him to narrate the events from an outsider's point of view. In these novels he elaborates the tension and conflict among the expatriates owing to their different identities. He is obsessed with the idea of presenting the chaos of inter-mixing of cultures. According to Bhabha:

The regulation and negotiation of those spaces that are continually, contingently, 'opening out', remaking the boundaries, exposing the limits of any claim to a singular or autonomous sign of differences where difference is neither one nor the other but something else besides that emerges in-between the claims of the past and the needs of the present. (219)

Sentiments of love and sex are hardly valued among the displaced colonials like Salim. He experiences a unique sense of ecstatic joy and satisfaction in his involvement with Yvette. His past experience of "brothel sex" has produced only contempt for himself and his partners. But his relationship with Yvette is invigorating in which he feels the emergence of a new self. As he is preoccupied with the idea of wining Yvette, he is frightened by a vision of the decay of the man he has known himself to be. After his serious involvement and disillusionment with Yvette, Salim realizes that had he "understood more about Raymond earlier, he might have seen Yvette more clearly her ambition, her bad judgment, her failure and would not have become involved with people as trapped as myself" (*A Bend in the River* 199).

Naipaul condemned orthodox Indian traditions and became agnostic and non-believer. He also regretted the lack of native traditions in Trinidad. He felt that the Indian immigrants in Trinidad lived in double exile. In his works, one finds recurrent themes of diasporic concerns and a psychology of marginalization, homelessness, spiritual isolation and perpetual exile. His creative talent has been shaped by continuous perception of rootlessness, deracination and displacement.

Naipaul's predicament of dislocation and alienation from his traditional history leaves him into a kind of cultural friction. The friction which he always wanted to cast off persists throughout his works. Naipaul feels comfortable and secure as a colonial in Trinidad therefore adopts an attitude which aims at pointing out the destitution and political and cultural mimicry of the Third World.

To conclude, in the above novels the writer is very close to have a rather mature outlook because now he finds the diasporic ambivalence prevailing everywhere in colonial world and imperial world. Naipaul here attains a universal understanding after his long stay in London and understanding the journeys in almost all the parts of the world. Understanding all his nostalgic diasporic longings and desire to belong either to Trinidad, India or England, now he defends assimilation of cultures, though it is quite an obscure idea for an expatriate. His defense of assimilation is based on his understanding of the postcolonial world after traveling far and wide. He seems to have reached to the conclusion that ambivalence, frustration, isolation, up-rootedness, alienation, homelessness and sense of insecurity are common traits in all cultures in the modern time and the search for stability is a burning issue due to politics of ethnicity.

Works Cites

Bhabha, Homi. *Nation and Narration*. London: Routledge, 1990. Print.

---. *Location of Culture*. London: Rutledge, 1994. Print.

---. “Dissemination: Time, Narrative and the Margins of the Modern Nation.” *Nation and Narration*. Ed. Homi Bhabha. London: Routledge, 1990. Print.

Boehmer, Elleke. *Colonial and Postcolonial Literature: Migrant Metaphors*. New York: Oxford University Press, 1995. Print.

Hall, Stuart. “Cultural Identity and Diaspora.” *Theorizing Diaspora: A Reader*. Ed. Jana Evan Braziel and Anita Mannur. London: Blackwell Publishing Ltd, 2003.

King, Bruce. *V. S. Naipaul*. London: Macmillan, 1993. Print.

--- . *Modern Novelist: V. S. Naipaul*. London: Macmillan Press, 1989. Print.

Loomba, Ania and Suvir Kaul, eds. *On India: Writing History, Culture, Post-Coloniality. Special Issue of Oxford Literary Review* 16.2 (1994): 23-34. Print.

Mittapalli, Rajeshwar and Micheal Hensen, eds. *V.S. Naipaul: Fiction and Travel Writing*. New Delhi: Atlantic, 2002. Print.

Mohan, Champa Rao. *Postcolonial Situation in the Novels of V. S. Naipaul*. New Delhi: Atlantic Publisher and Distributers, 2004. Print.

Naipaul, V. S. “Conrad’s Darkness.” *Critical Perspectives of V. S. Naipaul*. Ed. Robert D. Hammer. London: Heinimann, 1997. Print.

Naipaul, V.S. “Prologue to an Autobiography.” *Literary Occasions: Essays*. Ed. Pankaj Mishra. New Delhi: Picadore, 2003. Print.

Renan, Ernest. “What is a Nation?” *Nation and Narration*. Ed.Homi K. Bhabha.

London: Rutledge, 1990. Print.

Shuval, Judith. "Diaspora Migration: Definitional Ambiguities and a Theoretical Paradigm." *International Migration* 38.5 (2000): 41-56. Print.

CHAPTER FOUR

Caste, Ethnicity and Social Fragmentation in The Mimic Men and The Suffrage of Elvira

This chapter views some of the problems faced by the diasporic community due to their caste and ethnicity in the settled society as revealed in the novels of Naipaul. Almost all the diasporic communities face initial problems and sufferings, when they settle in a new land. Among the problems that diasporic communities face in the settled country are discrimination and social fragmentation. Discrimination is the leading trauma, which upsets them most, and caused a subaltern status in an alien land.

Caste and ethnicity as a factor for social discrimination in India remain one of the major concerns in Naipaul's writings. Since his childhood he observed indentured people sticking to the heritage of caste identity they brought from India. They take it as a means of protection according to Purbi Panwar:

They carried their faith in caste and creed with them and clung to them for security, in an alien world. Caste and religion had become an institution for them, which they thought would protect their identity. (108)

Naipaul argues that caste disparities construe its social structure so equality among the habitants would be a 'Utopian dream.' Naipaul had never been untouched by caste hierarchy. The hierarchy which withdraws him from India gave him a subject to deal social fragmentation in society.

Naipaul satirizes the dichotomy of India secularism. Indian is a secular and democratic country constitutionally but not so in real life. Dr. Radhakrishnan in *Religion and Society* asserts, "The aim of democracy is always the interest of society as a whole, not any class or community. All individuals immaterial of their race of religion have the right to an equal share in the political power of the society" (Radhakrishnan 91).

His writings are marked with the social and cultural friction among homeless people caused by ethnic traditions, while showcasing "failure of old and new system and rituals in the face of economic modernity" (Mustafa 2). Naipaul preferably narrates the bare truth of Africa and

Caribbean colonies and brings out "a conclusion" to put in Fauzia Mustafa's words, "about cultural and political poverty that seems to characterize an increasingly destitute greater third world" (3).

As a descendant of sugar plantation indentured family, Naipaul has been witnessing his forefathers' clinging to the age-old tradition and their denial of the new. Many of his books exploit same theme, where there is an apparent clash between the new and the old. He reinterprets "colonial history" and makes it an inseparably part of his expression. Naipaul bears his writings on postcolonial binary and explores the tension between the rich and the poor, colonized and the colonizer; powerless and powerful, centre and the margin.

Many times, even after adjusting in the new environment Naipaul's characters face several other problems such as ethnicity, discrimination, alienation and identity crisis. During the period of settlement in the new country, almost everyone in the diasporic community would undergo psychological trauma. Feeling of loss, sense of alienation from the society, loneliness and longing are a part of diasporic literature.

Naipaul's perspective begins with the non-Western person's realization of this state of the sense of having boundaries drawn around his life by the West. Having sensed this dispossession, the former colonial begins to fantasize, to dream of greater reality, and seeks to create the conditions of liberation. In his major fiction, Naipaul portrays marginalized characters on the basis of caste, ethnicity, class, nationality and color. They are understandable in terms of intersecting dialects of slavery and the impact of imperialism and colonization. Naipaul portrays men who cannot construct a coherent self and the reasons for this malady lie deep in the pattern of subordination and existential split suffered by them under a system that recognized no difference, humanly or culturally in its ruthless drive to hegemonies everything. As Peter Hughes has commented:

Above all, because the writing out of the narrative of decline and fall, of disorder and lack of authority involves the discovery of a void at the heart of Naipaul's world and it has been discovered through his writings. (31)

The Mimic Man presents more complex dilemma— the predicament of a colonial expatriate from an outsider's point of view. In this novel Naipaul depicts a newly independent country in the Caribbean, the island of Isabella. In spite of the long-cherished achievement of the independence, it appears that the previously colonized people of the island are unable to establish order and administer their country. The feelings of dislocation, place lessness, fragmentation and loss of identity haunt their psyche and thus they are reduced to the status of "mimic" men who imitates and reflect the colonizer's lifestyle, values and views.

The Mimic Men by V.S. Naipaul is a novel that revolves around the life of its protagonist, Ralph Singh. The novel is an autobiographical product of Ralph Singh where he collected the memoirs of his life. Ralph Singh is the perfect example of the mimic men. From Singh's narration the readers get an idea into his life and his surroundings, "in *The Mimic Men* Naipaul is primarily interested in the development of Singh's personality as he wrestles with the difficulty of finding reality, conditioned as he has been to settle for mimicry" (Boxill 12).

The novel examines the Island of Isabella, a newly independent country in the Caribbean. Though independent, the Island proved to be unable to offer its people any sense of identity or national unity. During the colonial period the colonizers have shaped richly the lives of people with its rich exuberant English 'modern' culture; but this modernity did not belong to the people of the Island. It was not something they could relate themselves to. That is why when the colonizers, the people of the Island came to know that they were into a world they do not recognize. They suffered from never-ending conflict, dislocation, place lessness, fragmentation and a loss of identity. To read the novel from a political or materialistic point of view is not enough, the psychological damage that is done is very evident in the book which cannot be ignored.

Mimicry is the outcome of colonization that started from the colonizing period and crept into the postcolonial era. A famous critic is of the view "An increasingly important term in postcolonial theory, because it has come to describe the ambivalent relationship between colonizer and colonized" (Griffith 124). The concept of mimicry is heavily discussed by Homi Bhabha where he says, "Colonial mimicry is the desire for a reformed, recognizable other, as a subject of a difference that is almost the same, but not quite" (122).

Oppression and frustration of the natives during the colonial period leads them to have firm belief that the whites and Europeans are superior and they were inferior. A blind imitation of the whites would lead them to superiority and an access to the powers they hold. Ralph Singh is the ultimate mimic man of Naipaul to whom London was a 'promised land' where he could search order. His attraction towards whiteness is revealed in the very first page of the novel when Singh expresses his opinions about the white man Mr. Shylock:

Suits made of cloth so fine I felt I could eat it. I had nothing but admiration. Mr. Shylock looked distinguished, like a lawyer or businessman. He had the habit of stroking the lobe of his ear and inclining his head to listen. I thought the gesture was attractive; I copied it. (*The Mimic Man* 7)

Bhabha also states though mimicry to the colonized is the "most elusive and effective strategies of colonial power and knowledge" (122). It leaves people more confused than ever "the discourse of mimicry is constructed around ambivalence" (122).

Bhabha also says that "mimicry repeats rather than represents" thus growth of an individual is not possible if one always haunts what he lacks which explains why at the end of the novel, Ralph Singh mimicry and an attraction towards the white, the English, the foreign disappoints him. Mimicry also becomes a hopeless attempt due to reasons elaborated later in this novel which explains the sufferings of the colonized people. Boxill exclaims, "How can a society which is profoundly mimic produce anything which is not itself mimic; how can a man who is not sure what he is produce anything which is genuinely his own?" (13)

Homelessness is a distinguished feature that emerges as a result of colonization. The protagonist, Ralph Singh suffers from the feeling of being homeless which gives rise to his identity crisis. Born in the Island of Isabella among people of multiple ethnicities he had always been detached from his original homeland, his country, India. During the period of colonial rule, the colonizers provided the people of the Island with the English world and presented the English way of life as a world of discipline, success and achievement. The colonizers have made these people believe that their English ways and manners were superior to the inferior natives of the Island. Ralph Singh grew up knowing the English world as an integral part and parcel of his life.

Thus, he took for granted that every culture was like the culture of the English and every world was a subset of the English world. Having no knowledge of his original culture and traditions, Singh viewed the world through the colonizers eyes and fantasized his own land to similar to the English lands. This is proved true when Singh imagines his grandmother "leading her cow through a scene of pure pastoral, calendar pictures of English gardens superimposed on our villages of mud and grass" (89).

On the other hand, the Island where he was brought up could not provide him with any (true) identity as well. The Island which was a melting pot of people of mixed race, mixed culture and traditions did not hold any significance for a particular religion or culture that even when Singh belonged to the ethnicity minority. Moreover, impressed by the English culture and lifestyle Singh could not relate himself to the variety of people having various conducts, cultures and histories. Singh had Chinese, Black and French people who were natives of the Island as friends.

Browne was among those people who could live contended by blending what has been provided by the colonizers and incorporating them into their native ways, that the "native and Western are linked" (Cooke 37). Browne wanted Singh to see that they had a history, though 'contrived' and 'manufactured, but the Island of Isabella did have some sort of history after all, if one wanted to search for it. He demonstrates emphatically:

Our landscape was manufactured as that of any great French or English park. But we walked in a garden of hell, among trees, some still without popular names, whose seeds had sometimes been brought to our island in the intestines of slaves. (Brown 147)

Browne was very optimistic about the idea that there were promising perspectives of the Island from which one can view the nodal points of this history, all they needed to do is to make this history their own "look above the roofs of the city and imagine!" (147). Browne persuaded Singh to come out of his 'classical' perspective and argued "the first task awaiting the islanders, to provide native names and thereby clarify the order which exists in indigenous terms, is implied" (Cooke 36). Singh had a more pessimistic view and he mockingly thought that "Browne's pretentiousness is actually a mask for his own discomfort" (Cooke 37).

Mostly in the early novels of Naipaul, England has been presented as the land of dream for the Trinidadian who find their own world to be incomplete, unreal and having no opportunity. Ganesh in *Mystic Masseur* and Anand in A *House for Mr. Biswas* escape to London to realize their cherished dreams. Their departure from the colonial land marks the end of these books. In the later phrase of literary career, Naipaul follows the expatriate's piquant tragedies by placing them in alien territories in the far-off lands and brings to the fore their intensified sense of ambivalence, loneliness, fear, a sense of futility, disappointment and mimicry in England as well as in Trinidad.

The Mimic Men reinforces Naipaul's shattered colonial fantasy of London and England, epitomes of European high culture and elitist cosmopolitanism. At the opening of the novel, during his first sojourn in London shortly after the war with all the compulsions and hopes driving him away from his native island of Isabella, Ralph Singh portrays his experience of all the insecurities and uncertainties as an immigrant. The Kensington boarding-house where he stays is owned by a Jewish landlord Mr. Shylock, "the recipient each week of fifteen times three guineas, the possessor of a mistress and of suits made of cloth so fine I felt I could eat it" (*The Mimic Man* 3). When he sees snow for the first time in his life, his feeling of expectation is colored by the awareness of disillusionment, and his mood shifts from the ecstatic to the morbid. The selection of his observation emphasizes the tensions:

Snow! At last; my element and these were flakes, the airiest crushed ice more than crushed shivered. But the greater enchantment was the light. Then I climbed up and up towards the skylight, stopping at each floor to look out at the street. The carpet stopped; the stairs ended in a narrow gallery. Above me was the skylight, below me the stair-well darkening as it deepened. The attic door was ajar. I went in, and found myself in an empty room harsh with a dead-fluorescent light that seemed artificial. The room felt cold, exposed and abandoned. The boards were bare and gritty. A mattress on dusty sheets of newspapers; a worn blue flannelette spread; a rickety writing-table. No more. (4-5)

Seeing the attic where Mr. Shylock used to live, Ralph Singh realizes "an analogy between the wandering, displaced Aryan and the homeless Jew, both cosmopolitans rejected by the societies in which they attempt to settle" (King 78).

There is a contrast between the beauty of the snow and the ugliness of the buildings and the bombsite. The tension of Ralph Singh's experience lies in the minute observation of the dinginess and shabbiness of the setting within which the perception and hope of absolute beauty occur. It predetermines his decisive failure in London later. He begins to question his irrelevance to the metropolis, "Yet what was I to do with so complete a beauty?" He felt all the magic of the city go away and had an intimation of the forlornness of the city and of the people who lived in it" (5). The mood of *The Mimic Men*, Ralph Singh's memoir, is thus established—the fusion of the moment of expected fulfilment and celebration with the knowledge of loss and desolation on both communal and individual levels.

Mr. Shylock's boarding-house also "called a private hotel" (3), ironically reminds the reader of the "Europeans Only" Earl's Court private hotel where Margaret stays in *Mr. Stone and the Knights Companion*, except that the boarding-house is a world of immigrants from different parts of the world. The christening party for the illegitimate child, mothered by the boarding-house's Maltese housekeeper Lieni and fathered by an Indian engineer, gives a clue about the "forlornness" of London and its inhabitants:

Other boarders came down. The girl from Kenya; her man friend, a blond, vacant alcoholic incapable of extended speech and making up for this with a fixed smile and gestures of great civility; the smiling, mute Burmese student; the Jewish youth, tall and prophetic in black; the bespectacled young Cockney who had as much trouble with his two Italian mistresses, according to Lieni, as with the police; the Frenchman from Morocco who worked all day in his room, kept to Moroccan temperature with a paraffin stove, translating full-length American thrillers at speed—he did one or two a month. (13)

Here, a tableau of ethnic diversity is painted. The heterogeneity and intermixture of immigrants with different cultural backgrounds instantly rise in visibility, suggesting a major demographic shift in the post-war metropolis.

Although Naipaul makes the hybrid experience in the historical context of transnational migration the primary ground for the intermingling of cultures and identities, he does not naively contend that mere coexistence of people of heterogeneous cultural, national, religious or other identity formations guarantees the uptake or expression of cosmopolitan openness. He is skeptical about people's cosmopolitan disposition—a conscious attempt to become familiar and engaged with others, and to be receptive to cultural outputs of others.

The Mimic Men discusses from the perspective of the immigrants how and why they restrain themselves from the mingling and fusion of the cultures of others. Like the English characters in *Mr. Stone and the Knights Companion*, the immigrants in London in *The Mimic Men* are not enthusiastic about experiencing joy or stimulation through immersing themselves in cultural differences either. They have only fear, suspicion and exclusion in their engagement with others. This seems to be an irony—the global migration has "contaminated" the larger world, while the immigrants themselves are not in praise of cosmopolitan contamination. In the novel, at the christening party for Lieni's baby, Lieni's Maltese friends "came in together and talked glumly in English and their own language" (12). Among the unequal elements of the boarding-house, the Maltese, enjoying immediate contacts with different cultures, encapsulate themselves in their territorial language and culture. Ralph Singh observes, "Conversation, apart from that conducted by the Maltese group, was not easy. We sat and waited for Lieni, whom we could hear in the kitchen" (13). But Lieni is virtually left in despair, she and her baby are abandoned by the engineer who has a wife and children in India. The abandonment ultimately undercuts and mocks the christening of the hybrid baby, a seeking for official sanction. Compared to the Maltese who do not step out of their ethnic clique, Ralph Singh seems more "cosmopolitan." He always picks out the Continental girls (Norwegian, Swedish, French and German Swiss) in his sexual encounters in London. However, his involvement is superficial. He confesses:

Both of us adrift in London, the great city. I with my past, my own darkness, she has no doubt with hers. Always at these moments the talk of the past, the landscapes, their familiar settings which I wished them to describe and then feared to hear about. I never wished even in imagination to enter their Norman farmhouse or their flats in Nassjo, pronounced Neshway, or their houses set atop the rocky fiords of geography books. I never wished to hear of the relationships that bound them to these settings, the pettiness by which they had already been imprisoned. I never wanted our darkness, our auras, to mingle. (*The Mimic Man* 24)

Like the Maltese, Ralph Singh refuses an open stance toward others as well. His random interracial sexual liaisons, which show "his inability to be part of or to lose himself in someone or some group beyond himself" (King 74), force upon him alienation, bewilderment and corruption.

What restrains Ralph Singh's cosmopolitan impulse is his inborn and enclosed in Hindu system of racial and cultural purity alerting him to the potential danger of hybridity. For Naipaul, as long as the immigrants lack cosmopolitan openness in their dealing with cultural diversity and otherness, the cosmopolitanism that they ostensibly epitomize in the form of hybridity cannot be a state of readiness searching for contrasts rather than uniformity.

In his confession of the anxious nature of his interracial sexual failures, Ralph Singh forms a new connection—his pursuit of sex and his disillusionment with London. His awareness of the social isolation within which he exists is evident:

How right our Aryan ancestors were to create gods. We seek sex, and are left with two private bodies on a stained bed. The larger erotic dream, the god, has eluded us. It is so whenever, moving out of ourselves, we look for extensions of ourselves. It is with cities as it is with sex. We seek the physical city and find only a conglomeration of private cells. In the city as nowhere, else we are reminded that we are individuals, units. Yet the idea of the city remains; it is the god of the city that we pursue, in vain. (*The Mimic Man* 17)

As Peggy Nightingale observes the god of the city that Ralph Singh searches for is "the god who would unite individuals in a common order" (100). Rather he experiences London as a private nightmare of intensified alienation and loneliness:

Here was the city, the world. I waited for the flowering to come to me. The trams on the Embankment sparked blue. The river was edged and pierced with reflections of light, blue and red and yellow. Excitement! Its heart must have lain somewhere. But the god of the city was elusive. The tram was filled with individuals, each man returning to his own cell. The factories and warehouses, whose exterior lights decorated the river, were empty and fraudulent. I would play with famous names as I walked empty streets and stood on bridges. But the magic of names soon faded. Here was the river, here the bridge, there that famous building. But the god was veiled. My incantation of names remained unanswered. In the great city, so solid in its light, which gave color even to un-rendered concrete—to me as colorless as rotting wooden fences and new corrugated-iron roofs—in this solid city life was two-dimensional. (18)

London— "the great city, center of the world" (17), the symbol of colonial hope and promise—is shown as a scene of lost and abandoned individuals, lonely and helpless in distress. The physical greatness of the metropolis that has nothing to do with the colonials/immigrants only reminds them of their powerlessness. In John Clement Ball's words, "The phantasmic metropolis that Ralph Singh experiences highlights the dissolution of community into atomized individuals and dissolves individuals into nothingness" (145-46).

Ralph Singh's feeling of rootless isolation is a common experience shared by the ethnically segregated immigrants. They are shunned by the host society, have no community to fall back on, and at the same time are afraid of stepping out of their home culture to get involved with others. Similarly, Naipaul writes about his early London life in *An Area of Darkness*:

Here I became no more than an inhabitant of a big city, robbed of loyalties, time passing, taking me away from what I was, thrown more and more into myself. All mythical lands faded, and in the big city I was confined to a smaller world than I had ever known. I became my flat, my desk, my name. (*An Area of Darkness* 38)

In *The Mimic Men*, the immigrants' forced status of being unattached in their two-dimensional metropolitan life provides an "advantage" for them. They can invent their identity as they wish. As Ralph Singh tells the reader, "There was no one to link my present with my past, no one to note my consistencies or inconsistencies. It was up to me to choose my character" (*The Mimic Men* 19). To compensate for their anonymity in the metropolis, the immigrants offer "simple versions of themselves" (13) by reference to upper-class, European respectability.

In Isabella since his childhood, Ralph Singh knows that "it was a disgrace to be poor" (*The Mimic Men* 89). Although he sympathizes with his alienated father (a poor schoolteacher), he prefers to lay claim to his mother's family. His mother's family is "among the richest in the island" and belongs to a small group known as "Isabella millionaires" (89). They own the Bella Bella Bottling Works, and are the local bottlers of Coca-Cola. They sponsor two popular radio programmes, and organize schoolchildren to visit their factory, distributing free Coca-Colas at the end of these educational tours.

As Margaret imitates her social superior (Tomlinson) in *Mr. Stone and the Knights Companion*, Ralph Singh is attracted to Sandra, a white English schoolmate. Sandra's Englishness outweighs Ralph Singh's Indo-Caribbean identity. Her elitist cosmopolitan taste outshines his dandy persona. Sandra's enjoyment of consumption satisfies Ralph Singh's colonial fantasy of how elitist cosmopolitanism should exist in the metropolis. He views his alliance with her elitist cosmopolitan taste as an alliance with the metropolitan attributes of ambition, spirit and an avid celebration of life. But the fact that Ralph Singh overlooks is when Sandra asks him to marry her, she is just uncertain about her future in London. Having failed a qualifying examination, the route of escape from the commonness through education is no longer available to her. Returning to the colonial milieu of Isabella where she can enjoy a privileged position with Ralph Singh, the dandy she at least can still play her persona as an elite cosmopolitan. The marriage has nothing to do with love or respect from the start.

If London is the testing ground for Ralph Singh's colonial fantasy, Isabella is the testing ground for Sandra's elitist cosmopolitanism. Upon the couple's return to Isabella, their mixed marriage is instantly shunned by Ralph Singh's maternal family. But they do not care, because they soon find it easy and comfortable to operate in a "neutral, fluid" group of people similar to themselves:

The men were professional, young, mainly Indian, with a couple of local whites and colored; they had all studied abroad and married abroad; on Isabella they were linked less by their background and professional standing than by their expatriate and fantastically cosmopolitan wives or girlfriends. Americans, singly and in pairs, were an added element. It was a group to whom the island was a setting; its activities and interests were no more than they seemed. There were no complicating loyalties or depths; for everyone the past had been cut away. (*The Mimic Men* 57)

With the passage of time, the elite cosmopolitans in Isabella in *The Mimic Men* eschew the local people and culture in favor of the perceived global standards of excellence. Ralph Singh and Sandra grow apathetic to the beauty of Isabella after listening to their friends' pastoral odes to the West—the sunset in Mississippi, the snow in Prague, and the English Midland landscape at dusk. The sense of place and community—an assemblage of fragments and a shared fantasy—of the cosmopolitans in Isabella is forged through their sense of themselves as the elite, as travelers, as touched by the charm and magic of worldliness and metropolitan life. The power of the myth of the metropolitan center further displaces the periphery. Later, when all the consumption activities in self-repetitions become boring, the elite cosmopolitans begin to complain about "the narrowness of island life: the absence of good conversation or proper society, the impossibility of going to the theatre or hearing a goodsymphony concert" (69). Thomas F. Halloran comments:

The pastorals of the centre—the cosmopolitan voice that critiques Isabella's lack of centres of national and cultural arenas—exemplify the power of Western writing to influence the imagination of the colony and create a hierarchy of culture, whereby the colony defines itself on the colonizer's terms. This construction is particularly powerful because it is the colonized who lust for Western commodities and traditions. (124)

Sandra's ethnocentric illiberal attitude toward race further exposes the fraudulence of elitist cosmopolitanism. When the cosmopolitan charm wanes in Isabella and commonness engulfs her again, Sandra begins to assert a higher view of herself through a contemptuous labelling of others, according to their national or racial background. She pejoratively calls her Swedish friend "common little Lapp", a Dutch girl who marries to a Surinamese "subkraut", and a Latvian girl "sub-Asiatic" (68), among all, Isabella is "the most inferior place in the world" full of "inferior expats" (71).

Ralph Singh feels more and more uncomfortable with her "fixed judgements and attitudes" (68). In his eyes, when the metropolitan certainty that he seeks in Sandra is shown to be nothing more than emptiness and ennui, she becomes as vulnerable as himself in London. When the desperate self-defense behind her fake elitist cosmopolitanism becomes clear, she becomes superfluous. Sandra soon leaves Ralph Singh for Miami with her American lover. The quick failure of their marriage (a pattern of dependence and pretension) symbolizes the infeasibility of the metropolitan, elitist model of cosmopolitanism in the Third World.

Ralph Singh's business success leads him into the local politics for Isabella's independence. Unlike his cosmopolitan friends, he actually participates in the local milieu. But this involvement further dehumanizes him, and eventually confirms his disillusionment with his colonial fantasy. Ralph Singh argues that politicians on the whole are hollow people clinging to some form of artificial power to create the illusion of success through manipulation:

Politicians are people who truly *make something out of nothing* (my emphasis). They have few concrete gifts to offer. They are not engineers or artists or makers. They are manipulators; they offer themselves as manipulators. Having no gifts to offer, they seldom know what they seek. They might say they seek power. But their definition of power is vague and unreliable. Is power the chauffeured limousine with fine white linen on the seats, the men from the Special Branch outside the gates, the skilled and deferential servants? But this is only indulgence, which might be purchased by anyone at any time in a first-class hotel. The politician is more than a man with a cause, even when this cause is no more than self-advancement. (*The Mimic Men* 37)

Ralph Singh observes that colonial politicians, in fear of losing the abstract power, push their bluff further in frenzy. In Isabella, colonial politicians are puppets manipulated through the Queen's representative, the Governor, numerous English expatriates who "virtually monopolized the administrative section of our civil service" (228), and higher technical experts on short-term contracts. They cannot stand on their own in the "fragmented, inorganic" society where real powers "come from the outside" (224). Their unstable foundation rests with the metropolitan centre.

The biggest development that Naipaul makes in *The Mimic Men* is that he for the first time reflects on the corrosive, damaging effect of colonial education on the sensibility of students, especially students like Ralph Singh and the colonial politicians who enter the elite strata of the society. Colonial education brings about escapism and fantasy, and leads them to hollow mimicry and a denial of their environment and of themselves. In his 1964 article "Jasmine", Naipaul criticizes the built-in alienating effect of the formal practice of studying English literature. It divorces a reader from relating literature to real life and breeds experiential separation.

There is a distinct dichotomy in their life at school and outside of school. They choose to withdraw into the private but unreal sphere of school life, banishing actual everyday life. In doing so, they are further alienated and fragmented, as Ralph Singh combines fantasy and reality together:

In my imagination I saw my mother's mother leading her cow through a scene of pure pastoral: calendar pictures of English gardens superimposed on our Isabella a village of mud and grass: village lanes on cool mornings, the ditches green and grassy, the water crystal, the front gardens of thatched huts bright with delicate flowers of every hue. She was as brightly colored a storybook figure as her husband. (95)

Although Naipaul makes transnational migration in the form of hybridity the primary ground for the intermingling of cultures and identities, he does not naively contend that mere coexistence of people of heterogeneous cultural, national, religious or other identity formations in the metropolis guarantees the uptake or expression of cosmopolitan openness. Probably because of his own immigrant experience, he is skeptical about the immigrants' capability to float above the bounded-ness of their primordial communities and national fantasies.

The most important step that Naipaul has taken in *The Mimic Men* is his reflection on the damaging effect of colonial education, which builds unreal colonial fantasy and leads the colonials to hollow mimicry of the elite. Presenting the process of Ralph Singh's disillusionment, Naipaul suggests that only the realistic knowledge of both the First World and the Third World can lead the colonials out of their colonial shell. Ralph Singh's final acceptance of exile as a universal human condition is in accord with Naipaul's criticism of the immigrants' self-encapsulation: to enact the cosmopolitan identity project, the incompatibility between nomadic ideals and the countervailing desire for meaningful connections to people and places, a sense of communal belonging and stable, comfortably familiar routines has to be overcome.

The Suffrage of Elvira not only exploits the prevalent caste system but it also depicts underlying racism and persisting class conflicts in a multiracial and multicultural society. The novel reveals his understanding of the local scene and his capacity to reinforce with comic irony. *The Suffrage of Elvira* poses the distortions of personality and corruption of an individual under the pressure of reality. It also poses the societal level by exposing the distortion of such concepts as democracy and independence and the large-scale corruption of the society. The novel demonstrates Naipaul's "gift of atomizing the experience of a community into the intransigent particulars of colonial action and finally draws our attention from the community to the individuals who constitute it" (Madhusudana 15).

Naipaul traces the awakening of the people of "Elvira State" in this novel and brings to a focus the prospects and possibilities harbored by democracy in a corrupt and dishonest society— a maze of deals and inducements. And before going to explore what democracy in Elvira is as Naipaul represents it, it is worthwhile to note what he has to say on the political situation pervading in Trinidad or any other society around that time:

> Nationalism was impossible in Trinidad. In the colonial society every man had to be for himself; every man had to grasp whatever dignity and power he was allowed; he owed no loyalty to the island and scarcely any to his group. To understand this is to understand the squalor of the politics that came to Trinidad in 1946 when, after no popular agitation' universal adult suffrage was declared. The privilege took the population by surprise. The new politics were reserved for the enterprising, which had seen the prodigious commercial possibilities. There were no parties, only individuals. Corruption, not unexpected, aroused only amusement and even mild approval. (*The Middle Passage* 78)

Given this analysis and also what Naipaul says very early in the novel about the prospects of democracy, it is easier to notice the distorted use to which the ideal of democracy is put:

> Democracy had come to Elvira four years before, in 1946 but it had taken nearly everybody by surprise and it wasn't untill1950, a few months before the second general election under universal adult franchise that people began to see the possibilities. (*The Suffrage of Elvira* 13)

The noveltalks of a pure political process and it also speaks of social and religious state of Elvira. The people of

Elvira share their buffoonery in common with the people of Miguel Street. Naipaul deliberately dwarfs them; he sees the Euro- American life style as the ideal mode to be followed. Therefore, his interpretation is rarely pleasant according to Satendra Nandan, "Of course the writer may not give a pleasant interpretation of his experience (that is his prerogative), but it is profoundly compelling one, often poignantly moving" (Trivedi 64).

In describing West Indian dependence upon other countries as models of democratic action, Eric Williams underlines the very concept of mimicry that Naipaul conceptualizes, "Political forms and social institutions were imitated rather than created, borrowed rather than relevant reflecting the forms existing in the particular metropolitan country from which they were derived" (501). Naipaul writes about the breakdown of religious values in Elvira thus:

Things were crazily mixed up in Elvira. Everybody Hindus, Muslims and Christians owned a Bible; the Hindus and Muslims looking on it, if anything with greater awe. Hindus and Muslims celebrated Christmas and Easter. Everybody celebrated the Muslim festival of Hosein. In fact, when Elvira was done with religious festivals, there were few straight days left. (*The Suffrage of Elvira* 66)

In a society like this, religion is no longer a matter of spirit but becomes something that could be exploited in a variety of ways to meet the ends of selfish people. The names of the Baksh children also are suggestive of the mixed-up nature of religion in Elvira. The Baksh chose Christian and Muslim names alternately for their children as if it were a concession to their environment. The boys were named Foam, Iqbal, Herbert, Rafiq, Chrles, and the girls, Carol and Zilla.

Money is the main value of the society, and those who obtain money by cunning or cleverness are applauded irrespective of the means by which they earned it. No one has any scruples—honesty, selflessness, sincerity have long since fled. It is in portraying such a society in its true colours that we see Naipaul's awareness of the Third-World malaise.

The novel is a dramatic account of the political awakening of the village of Elvira— remote, unconnected, and dingy. "Elvira" is the short form for the Elvira Estate "named after the wife of one of the early owners" (10-11) of cocoa estate. In this novel, as Anthony Boxill points outs, "Naipaul makes an elaborate attempt to make the disordered past more concrete" (31).

Naipaul presents both his politicians and the electorate as tricksters and exploiters. Democracy becomes merely a guise for self-advancement. The candidates do not have a policy for the platform. Harbans's strategy is to get the Hindus to vote for him and to persuade the Muslims to do so through Baksh. Though people talk about unity, religious and racial chauvinism always take precedence over ideology. The politicians, in fact, make the people more and more racially conscious to meet their ends. The bitterness that exists between Hindus and Muslims is nothing else but racial prejudice. For instance, when Chittarnjan gets onto a fight with Baksh, he says, "Every Hindus blood is pure blood" (114). He goes on: "Muslim is everything and Muslim is nothing . . .. Even Negro is Muslim" (114).

The novel records the experiences of Surajpat Harbans, a PWD contractor, and the owner of a quarry and a transport service named after him, who now wants to test his fortune in the elections. Though John Thieme and Landeg White describe Harbans as innocent repeatedly tricked and betrayed by the public. His sole aim is to win the elections. He submits himself to the exploitative demands of the people of Elvira. Harbans has to resort demeaning and corrupt practices to appease different kinds of people in Elvira. To get the Hindu votes he has to please Chittranjan by agreeing to marry his son to Chittaranjan's daughter, Nelly, though it never materialized. To get the Muslim votes away from his rival, Preacher. The election strategy of Harbans further includes distribution of petrol and rum vouchers, posters, and banners. Baksh demands two hundred dollars and a loudspeaker van and seventy-five dollars per month for his eldest son, Foam, who is to be the manager of the campaign.

Harbans's path to the legislative council is further complicated by the appearance of the two self-styled witnesses of Jehovah and the dog Tiger; this brings to a focus the crucial role that Obeah and black magic play in such societies which are not yet ready to come out of their ignorance and superstitious tendencies.

On the polling day, given the fickle nature of the people, Harbans has to see that they would not change their minds in the last minute. His men have to take care of the agents and clerks at the polling booths who would otherwise stagger the polling process. Some men of tried criminality have to be appointed to see that the ballot-boxes reach the warden's office without any problem. All these make him so desperate that he looks only "sad and absent minded" (192) even in the moment of triumph.

After the victory, Harbans leaves Elvira but reappears at the function arranged by Ramlogan, who intends to resent a case of whisky to the winning candidate. He appears in an outfit that transforms his appearance completely. He drives a different vehicle too, a brand new blue and lack Jaguar instead of the old Dodge lorry at the function, the crowd go berserk and set fire to his car, which is not even a week old. Greatly agitated Harbans says "Elvira, you a bitch" (206) a second time in the novel and he comes no more to Elvera. Harbans's repeated imprecation "Elvira, you a bitch" (206) can be taken to refer both to the person and to the town for, as Anthony Boxill notes, "Like the original Elvira, the village is a bitch in the way she seeks to sell herself over again to Harbans" (54). In addition, as Elvira murdered her child, so her spiritual heirs subvert democracy for a few dollars. The people of Elvira as well as Elvira are wantonly destructive.

It is the characterization which transforms *The Suffrage of Elvira* into a genuine and impersonal piece of criticism of a society that is just coming out of colonial rule but incapable of freeing itself from colonial influence. Naipaul "offers us a mock-biography of his society by exposing its middle-class manners and morals, its philistine coarseness and vulgarity" (Madhusudan 72). All these evils surface during the election time. Democracy, the chief ideal to usher in order and social equality, can only give rise to confusion and chaos. Elections tend to cause dissensions or worsen existing prejudices and rivalries among the individuals, races, and religions. The kind of notions these ignorant, mentally immature, and irresponsible people entertain about democracy and election are worth-noting.

Chittranjan's observation is that everybody wants bribe these days becomes an ironical comment on the beginnings of the concept of democratic equality. The novel is in fact a consistently satire treatment of the human absurdities that men are capable of performing in the name of ideology. Connivance and corruption consequently become common denominators for the rich and the poor alike.

To some like Mrs. Baksh, democracy and the gift of franchise stand as symptoms of bad times. Hence, she keeps on warning her people many times in the novel:

Nobody is listening to me. She said, 'Everybody just washing their foot and jumping in this democracy business. But I promise you, for all the sweet, it going to end damn sour. Is this election sweetness that sweetens you up, Baksh? But, see how this sweetness going to turn sour. See. (*The Suffrage of Elvira* 82)

The people of Elvira are anti-democratic in spirit and pay only lip service to democracy. To them, election is a carnival, and democracy a farce rather than a passion or a lasting value. The unity of masses proves to be a shaky one, not grounded on a genuine historical or social awareness.

Mazururs Baksh, the Muslim tailor is a man of power who starts and ends as a trickster. All his energies are directed to extract the largest possible bribe from Harbans in return for the promise of the Muslim vote. Though he has no dignity as a leader, he is popular among the Muslims, probably because he is a big talker. People call him "mouther." He also "mixed with everybody" (13). He has long been a swindler. Years before the election, he contrived fraudulent practices such as the shirt-making scheme in which he sold cheap, one-size shirts as exclusively tailored.

Chittranjan, the goldsmith, is the leader of the Hindus in Elvira. He is another power center in Elvira, a man aloof and stiff. He becomes an important figure in the local politics because he has control over three thousand Hindu votes and one thousand Hindu votes and one thousand Spanish votes:

As a Hindu Chittranjan naturally had much influence among the Hindus of Elvira; but he was more than the

Hindu leader. He was the only man who carried weight with the Spaniards of Cordoba (it was said he lent them money); many Negroes liked him; Muslims didn't trust him, but even they held him in respect. (*The Suffrage of Elvira* 24)

Chittranjan is a popular man in Elvira because he is rich and owns the biggest house in Elvira. In the election, Chittranjan is a staunch supporter of Harbans, and of course, he has his own selfish reason for it. He wants to marry his daughter Nelly to Harbans's son, though Harbans is not keen on this alliance. In spite of this Chittranjan chalks out all the election schedules and helps in devising certain strategies to win the votes such as taking care of the sick people of Elvira and providing monetary help to the poor and the sick.

Foam is another important figure in the election drama. He is the eldest son of Baksh. He works hard for Harbans in the elections, "He worked not so much for the victory of Harbans and the defeat of preacher, as for the humiliation of Lorkhoor and Teacher Francjis" (40). He is appointed the Campaign Manager at seventy-five dollars a month. He is a loyal and responsible supporter, unlike his deceitful father.

Lorkhoor, the childhood rival of Foam, is called by Teacher Francis as "a born writer." Teacher Francis helps him to become the star of the Elvara social and Debation Club as he is a talented boy with a gift of the gab and a creative hand. He secures the job of advertising for the cinema in a loudspeaker van through Teacher Francis which otherwise would have gone to Foam. This intensifies the enmity between them.

Lorkhoor acts as the campaign manager for preacher and betrays him in the end. He is self-centered and sells his votes to Harbans. Finally, he elopes with "doolahin," the daughter-in-law of Dhaniram, and leaves Elvira for good. Baksh and Lorkhoor reveal the self-centeredness and the centrifugalism inherent in the West Indian society, which surfaces at the time of elections.

Preacher, the Negro candidate is another eccentric character. He has the supporter of two thousand Negro votes besides some Spanish and Hindu votes wooed by Lorkhoor. He is "a tall Negro with high frizzy hair, long frizzy beard, and long white robe" (37). His campaigning includes energizing and long walking-tours with a Bible in one hand, and a stone in the other. He is not disheartened by his defeat, but goes round briskly from house to house, thanking the people. Once the elections are over, he fades into anonymity.

Dhaniram and Mahadeo are two other supporters of Harbans who play minor roles in the novel. They are included in the committee "only to keep them from making mischief" (42). Dhaniram is a Hindu pundit in Elvira who lives in a wooden bungalow with his paralyzed wife and his meek young daughter-in-law, who was deserted by Dhaniram's son just two months the marriage.

Thus, it is evident from the study of discussed novels that there is an overall atmosphere of despair among the characters of different caste and ethnicity in a fragmented society. The denizens of Central Africa can have no leap in the dark to a higher order of living as a permanent answer to existential anguish. And the novel explores the beleaguered identities of the colonized and the colonizers alike in two different landscapes—Caribbean and African. The work delineates the trauma of an Eastern African's displacement towards the bush culture and resultant confrontation between the natives and aliens on the basis of caste and ethnicity. These novels establish Naipaul as a novelist constantly evolving and exploring newer regions confronting certain colonial/postcolonial dichotomies.

Works Cited

Bhabha, Homi. *Nation and Narration.* London: Routledge, 1990. Print.

---. *Location of Culture.* London: Rutledge, 1994. Print.

Boxill, Anthony. *V. S. Naipaul's Fiction: In Quest of the Enemy.* New Brunswick: York Press, 1983. Print.

---. *The Little Bastard World of V. S. Naipaul's The Mimic Men* and *A Flag on the Island. Pdf.* Web. 04 Sep. 2012. 12-19.

Cooke, John. "A Vision of the Land: V. S. Naipaul's Later Novels." *Journal of Caribbean Studies* 24.1(1980): 140-61 Print.

Mustapha, Nasser. "The Influence of Indian Islam on Fundamentalist Trends in Trinidad and Tabogo." *The Indian Diaspora: Dynamics of Migration.* Ed. N. Jayaram. New Delhi: Sage Publication, 2004. Print.

Panwar, Purabi. *V. S. Naipaul: An Anthology of Recent Criticism.* Delhi: Pencraft International, 2003. Print.

CHAPTER FIVE

CONCLUSION

V. S. Naipaul is one of the finest writers of English prose over the world and famous for his critical tone and piquant style of narration. He is an expert writer of exploiting each moment into literature. Basically, Naipaul is associated with the literature of "Diaspora" but in this book he has been established as a voice of subaltern, diasporic and marginalized people within postcolonial context. His oeuvre commonly speaks of expatriation, exile and the people who have been sidelined and discriminated from the society due to caste, class, gender and ethnicity. The issues like gender, diaspora, marginalization, subaltern and politics of ethnicity have been talked much at length in Naipaul's chosen texts.

The book projects subaltern and diaspora literature as a major part of postcolonial historiography. It also incorporates the voice of the people of inferior rank or position in fragmented discourse on caste, class, gender, ethnicity, subaltern and tribals in diasporic location. The dynamics of dominance and hierarchies within the groups, community's nation and gender was critiqued by Gayatri Spivak and Benedict Anderson. The main finding of the research is that so far in the categorization of subaltern groups the inclusions of people in the diaspora due to any reasons have not been established by the critics of subaltern studies in postcolonial theory. It created many ambiguities and paradoxes because the displaced people, by any reason, are the victim of marginalization against the issue of nationality and boundaries.

In recent years the increasing focus on the diaspora studies demonstrates the narratives and discourse of nation state. Focusing primarily on the land of origin/adoption binaries, the subject position of the natives in the diaspora literature is the suggestive of the new category of subaltern studies putting the issues of belongingness and un-belongingness at the centre. The home and (Un) home are contested categories within the postcolonial subaltern and diaspora discourse.

This book has discussed various representations of subaltern and diaspora within postcolonial set up in Naipaul's writings. Subaltern metaphors appear frequently, reflecting Naipaul's prominent literary themes. The subaltern metaphors in Naipaul's writings are often associated with the fictional characters' quest for freedom, identity and for a counter-force to social restrictions. As we have seen, Naipaul depicts a claustrophobic atmosphere to symbolize his characters' frustration and alienation when their sense of freedom remains unsatisfied. The whole Caribbean Island is described as a shipwreck to suggest a restrictive milieu.

In postcolonial literature, the representation which is prominent in Naipaul's writing is the dichotomic division between centre and margin. As the scholar has suggested in his argument, there is a chronological shift in Naipaul's representation of this dichotomic concept. His earlier phase shows the dichotomous division between centre and margin. While 'centre' embodies the location of freedom, security, and civilization, 'margin' symbolizes the location of cultural degradation. Yet in his later phase, Naipaul barely represents a categorically dichotomic view. Instead, he becomes more understanding towards the mixing of cultures and cultural hybridity.

To evaluate Naipaul's relationship with the dichotomic division is a complex matter. From a postcolonial perspective, the binary view of the world is problematic and should be deconstructed. In this light, Naipaul's works which occasionally reproduce a dichotomous view of the world are not entirely successful. However, the condition of Naipaul's subaltern representation lies in its complexity. He exposes his own view in showing that he has inherited the dichotomous diasporic view through the ideology of imperialism, and that has stubbornly remained with him. In other words, Naipaul reveals that imperialism is responsible for influencing his ideas and that the wrongs of a colonial education produced a persistent impact on the minds of colonial subjects.

In addition to Naipaul's subaltern depictions in his works, the book has also discussed Naipaul's own relationship with diasporic consciousness. It analyzed his journey, between Trinidad, England, and other countries that he has visited, and discussed Naipaul's life as a traveler and his view of the world. Here is revealed the essence of his rootlessness. Naipaul's relationship with rootlessness exposes the ambiguity in his work, while pursuing his quest to achieve greater freedom. He is, at times, nostalgic for a sense of belonging. Generally speaking, in the earlier phase of his time in England, Naipaul seemed to be uncomfortable with his sense of rootlessness. However, in his later career, Naipaul has become more comfortable with the idea of rootlessness.

Naipaul's relationship with diaspora, space, place, and movement can largely be explained within the context of the following terms: paradox, in-betweenness, ambiguity, and complexity. For instance, in spite of his openly expressed unwillingness to return, in his fictional works with a Trinidadian setting, Naipaul ambiguously expresses his mixed sentiment of compassion and detachment. Another ambiguity is seen in Naipaul's sense of belongingness, while he learns to accept and feels more comfortable with his rootless condition and paradoxically, he develops a greater sense of belonging to England. Naipaul's treatment of a dichotomous view of the world is also complex. He reproduces their perspective but at other times opposes its logic.

Naipaul has remained persistently devoted to his own colonial experiences in Trinidad. He has rightly been termed as a literary navigator for his portrayal of some of the world's old colonies hitherto unexplored by many Westerners. His pursuit for discovery and investigation earned Naipaul the recognition throughout his career. In post-colonial world, the task of third world writers become more challenging as it requires a higher level of sensitivity to highlight the discrepancies between inhabitants of the powerful and the powerless worlds. The various perspectives that Naipaul provides in his books enrich postcolonial writing and grant it a relishing flavor by discovering with great compassion the dilemma of the exile, the pain of homelessness and of loss of tradition.

He primarily presents a consistent image of social reality in the non-Western world, where dispossessed people search for order in their lives, he does not ignore the callousness and monotony in the lives of the Westerners.

Therefore, he is one of the most talked about and controversial Indian Diasporic writers in contemporary world. He rewrites and restates his place in the world history. His books defy all traditional norms of perception; on the contrary they offer a new and shocking yet real perception. In the present research an attempt to explore and establish him as a cosmopolitan writer has been made.

These paradoxes and ambiguities are significant factors in Naipaul's works. The paradoxes reflect the complexity of Naipaul as a former colonial subject whose origins were multi-cultural, and who acquired a multiple self. Naipaul's subaltern depiction is unique in its complexity and significant in today's multicultural society.

Naipaul's work presents a clear and distinctive conception of the relationship between the individual and his social environment, past and present. He has moved beyond preoccupation with the West Indians' special relationship to colonialism and an awakening collective social consciousness of that area, to offer perspectives on many facets of the larger world. He has approached his themes and topics, such as homelessness, cultural confusion, alienation, with a concept of the importance of universality. The range, however, is more often wide than deep. The Indian segment of Trinidad remains the only society which he portrays with intensive depth and artistic confidence. Nevertheless, his efforts to demonstrate the urgency of the problems that affect colonial and ex-colonial territories, the "unimportant", neglected places, as he calls them, convey persistent concerns. It has often been remarked that Naipaul is too much of a detached observer to effectively represent regions where the human history is controversial, personal crises and powerful. The author, nevertheless, in an article called "The Writer" published as early as 1966 in *The New Statesman*, states his belief that it is impossible to think of a writer, a novelist as being anything but attached. In this respect, the development of his work reveals a commitment to using his art as an instrument for analyzing and commenting on the human condition.

There are so many Indian writers writing in English like Mulk Raj Anand and R. K. Narayan. They talked about India in a mild ironic way but their approach is nowhere marked with disgust like Naipaul. It is true about Naipaul that he directly comments on the age-old practices which have lost their values and importance and seems irrelevant to him today. Tabish Khair bears a different opinion about Naipaul as he writes in Babu Fiction:

The twin fact that Naipaul unlike, say, Aubrey Menon or Sam Selvon— tends to write about India and diasporic Indians and gains visibility partly as an "Indian English" writer forces us to address his fiction. Even his reputation as an "expert" on India that Indians stems from the subject matter and impact of Naipaul's fiction for Naipaul is otherwise known as a Caribbean subject who has now become an English citizen. He has little knowledge of Indian language and cannot claim to be a scholar in, say, the fields of Asian or Indian studies. (Khair 244)

Like nations all over the world, the postcolonial societies of the West Indies are engaged in a struggle to resist and liberate themselves from centuries of imperial and social oppressions. Several of the writers have tried, through their art, to come to terms with the effects of this struggle and to portray the complex and painful adjustments that individuals are called upon to make in response to the changing conditions around them. Their works have dealt adequately with issues such as the exploitative colonial structures, the growth of a commercial middle class and the philistine societies of post-independence. The values often asserted by such writers are those of a national, independent, anti-colonial set-up. The emphasis has been on the reconciliation of the West Indian character to his history-the experiences of his past, with the hope of eradicating the all-pervasive sense of individual and communal alienation.

The writer presents dispossessed people who search for order in their lives. His postmodern and postcolonial status leads him to focus mainly on the problem of contemporary world struggling with the question with identity and Naipaul deviates from this question. In his wide range of writing, he covers up almost all the continents of the world as his travel is worldwide. He expresses candidly what he felt during those travels which aroused fervor all over the world. Africa is one of his favorites and most written about landscapes. He differs from the native's writings of Africans in his opinion. He does not believe in writing back to Europe as Achebe or Soyinka did, rather his attitude becomes Pro- Conradian in his depiction of the political and social situations of the continent. He talks about Africa as the land of action and violence and darkness. Naipaul follows the "imperialistic explanation of the world" (Boehmer 237). The issue of marginality, ambiguity, disintegration and mimicry form the core of Naipaul's narratives. The difficulty to understand one another's communicational gap, cultural distance and different occupy his themes.

Naipaul's self-reliant and self-sufficient nature grants him laxity to pass fierce and reckless remarks on his contemporaries and even on the famous Indian writers like R. K. Narayan or Mulk raj Anand. In an online interview with Farrukh Dhondy on Indanedione, he comments on "the pretense in Indian writing" that no, he doesn't think R. K. Narayan exalted his material or that Mulk Raj Anand, writing in the thirties and later, did. He thinks it occurred with the latest crop of writers, who have been encouraged by all kinds of foolish people to do these family sagas, and it's so bad for India, the encouragement of this rubbish.

The narratives of exile/migration or the fragmentation of the postcolonial self is no doubt, the result of colonialism that not only has shattered the geography and demography of the colonized lands but also the colonized self as well. Again, this fragmentation detaches or distances the colonial subject from the possibility of achieving a sense of reality or stability of the self. In *A Way in the World* (1994), Naipaul writes about the uncertainty of the life and existence of the Indian migrants:

Most of us know the parents or grandparents we come from. But we go back and back, forever; we go back all of us to the very beginning; in our blood and bone and brain we carry the memories of thousands of beings . . . Sometimes, we can be strangers to ourselves. (*A Way in the World* 9)

Thus, the migrants are strangers not only to the places they move in, but also, they are aliens to themselves. Naipaul's travels have made him so unsettled that no other writers of the colonial background feel so much dislocated not only with his own self but also with his theme and subject-matter. "Few writers even in the modern times of widespread migrancy," writes Harish Trivedi "could have inherited a sensibility so widely dislocated and so deeply disjointed as V. S. Naipaul" (*Journal of Caribbean Studies*).

Naipaul has been fiercely attacked and criticized for his fearless remark on India, Islam and religion but he never paid heed to them. No amounts of petitions have been able to change his tone and gesture. He still stands tall with his bitter and true remarks on the taboos of the world. His voice is difficult to silence. Due to his overpowering nostalgia and "ambiguous" historical origin Naipaul probably has a dearth of ideas which is obvious in thematic repetition in his books.

It is quite appropriate to state that Naipaul has maintained his distinction in this project as a writer writing for subaltern people in diaspora location because of his first-hand observation of the postcolonial "universal civilization" and his tendency to fearless present the gloom of the colonized and the colonizer alike, without bothering about his critics who call him a conniver against the Third World. As he has stayed long in London, he finds his traditions, nativity and language eroding with the passage of time. Naipaul observes that every writer, in the long run, has a tradition of his own. But in his case, he has no tradition to stick to. Moreover, he has been successful in making a special room for himself as a postcolonial writer because of his "universality" and objectivity of expression.

The book is divided into six chapters including conclusion. The first chapter i.e., Introduction deals with the critical survey of postcolonial literature and its many aspects like subaltern and diaspora in terms of caste, class, gender and location. The introduction chapter of the book provides a detailed understanding of the impact of subaltern and diaspora literature under postcolonial umbrella. Critics like Gayatri Chakravarty Spivak, Antonio Gramsci and Ranajit Guha have been discussed with their texts at length to expound the subaltern discourse. No doubt postcolonial is a big sea and one becomes '*other*' in one's country and here begins the process of 'otherization'. One feels '*other*' because of caste, class and gender. One has to face discrimination in society on the basis of outsider, caste, ethnicity and gender. The book also throws light on the scenario in which a person becomes subaltern in a diaspora location.

The second chapter entitled "Gendered Subalternism and Myth of Masculinity" deals with imbalance discourse in the proceeding novels such as *A House for Mr. Biswas, Half a Life and Magic Seeds.* In this chapter Naipaul made an attempt to explore major female characters like Shamas, Sarojini and Dehuti and their psychological states of mind seasoned with patriarchy. A strong gender bias has been felt in Naipaul's treatment and projection of female characters widely displays two broader categories of female characters— dominating and their subordinates. Regardless of their position in society they have a very little to say in their husband's lives.

Naipaul draws the distinction as a major setback for the progress of Indians in an alien and heterogeneous society. A feminist analysis brings out the untouched aspect of gender present in Naipaul's novels. In Indian society the female characters in Naipaul's novels are secondary, unsympathetic character and remain on margin. Thus, they have suffered doubly unlike women of the white world. They have suffered first on account of their race and class and then gender.

"Politics of Ethnicity and Subaltern Voices" is third chapter and Naipaul's Indian trilogy has been analyzed with unraveling observations on India. It highlights the soaring wounds which shattered his image of India. It brings Naipaul's attitude towards India and justifies his natural contempt for Indian culture and its people. The researcher reveals the instances where Naipaul's myth regarding India has been shattered. It is an answer to Naipaul's bitter and pungent reaction to Indian life style. In his famous Indian trilogy— *An Area of Darkness, Indian: A Wounded Civilization* and *India: A Million Mutinies Now,* Naipaul meticulously scrutinizes and demythologizes Indian culture. His myths of India as a golden land, as a dream destination, as a proud lineage were all demolished in one blow of reality hitting on the front. It made him almost hysterical, which he took years to come out of. Consequently, his writings on India bear negative trait.

The book reveals Naipaul's narrow view and mean remarks about Indian culture without considering the real significance. George Lamming states that his "Eurocentric attitude" is responsible for his scorn. He is thus bound to evaluate "orient" from a European parameter. It leads to disappointment and distress for an "insider-outsider" person like Naipaul.

Naipaul's using derogatory words for India and her culture shows his trick to present the nation as a land of primitives and serpent charmer before the eyes of western for the sake of getting name and fame. While using Indian myth Naipaul hardly bothers about the importance of those myths. He has done this intentionally as a politics to lower India's image and win laurels for himself.

The fourth chapter "*In a Free State* and *A Bend in the River:* The Psychology of Marginalization in Diasporic Location" deals with diasporic concerns and a psychology of marginalization in diasporic location. In these novels, one can see the postcolonial disorder, inter-tribal conflicts and the problems of identity because the characters of these novels are diasporic and marginalized. Both these novels offer "somber accounts of chaos at the time of the African transition to post colonialism, foregrounding the lack of a coherent ideology or leadership that might fill the vacuum left by the old political order" (Hawley 307-8). Both the novels depict Naipaul's vision of a free and fair world whose inhabitants might rise above the barriers of nation or nationality, and might consider themselves as the citizens of the world.

The paradoxes and ambiguities are significant factors in Naipaul's works. The paradoxes reflect the complexity of Naipaul as a former colonial subject whose origins were multi-cultural, and who acquired a multiple self. Naipaul's subaltern depiction is unique in its complexity and significant in today's multicultural society.

Chapter five is "Caste, Ethnicity and Social Fragmentation in *The Suffrage of Elvira* and *The Mimic Men.*" This chapter is a modest attempt to view some of the problems faced by the diasporic community due to their caste and ethnicity in the settled society. Almost all the diasporic communities face initial problems and sufferings when they settle in a new land. Among the problems that diasporic communities face in the settled country are discrimination and social fragmentation. Discrimination is the leading trauma, which upsets them most. The plants when plucked from a soil and planted in a new one has survival problem; similarly, the diasporic community too faces problem of survival. They have to adjust to the environment, language, culture and the society.

The writer presents dispossessed people who search for order in their lives. His postmodern and postcolonial status leads him to focus mainly on the problem of contemporary world struggling with the question with identity and Naipaul deviates from this question. In his wide range of writing, he covers up almost all the continents of the world as his travel is worldwide. He expresses candidly what he felt during those travels which aroused fervor all over the world.

To conclude, V. S. Naipaul's fiction undergoes certain paradigmatic shifts especially in the presentation of the representative subaltern and diasporic ambivalence among certain protagonists and other characters. His fiction is a parallel journey signifying his personal growth and ultimate mature perception. His treatment of the theme of "subaltern" under postcolonial umbrella is penetrating and comprehensive as he shares the anguish of colonial expatriates throughout his career. His novels are not merely reflections of abstraction; rather, they are packed with thought.

Naipaul's writings highlight the experiences of non-western peoples who have been uprooted by historical currents. Both considerate and critical he brings to light the failures of developing societies in the postcolonial era. Given the formlessness of their lives, such people seek to find order. How their struggle spread out becomes not merely a regional or racial narrative, but a human one. Within postcolonial hangover, writing as a dispossessed person, the one who has been culturally uprooted and forced to create his own world, Naipaul not only presents but also shares subjective perception. He finds personal reverberation with the worldview of the dispossessed former colonial subject who is busy in the pursuit of establishing their individual identity.

The conclusion brings into sharp focus the diverse patterns of ambivalence underlying existential search of a portion for the earth that runs beneath Naipaul's fictional works from the beginning to end. An analysis is made as how the past, in Naipaul's fiction, asserts itself through appreciation of tradition and how the former colonial subjects, dispossessed of their native tradition, are obsessed with regaining a distinctive identity. His travels along with his personal experience of rootlessness, made him emphatic in presenting the alienating effects of colonial past on today's postcolonial people.

The book observes Naipaul's personal displacement from his birth place for a settled life abroad and his consequent enigma of arrival in London as an expatriate making the lives of all the protagonists in his fiction. His aspirations connected to a "promised land" end in a deep sense of anguish and disillusionment that gets reflected in his works produced in different phases of his literary career. Thus, his journey as a prominent diasporic writer writing about subaltern people in terms of caste, class and gender, perhaps, ends as a writer with a high sense of maturity.

The book has been developed on the basis of the discourse of subaltern where the characters in Naipaul are put into category of subaltern on the basis of their caste, class and gender. However, subalternism in Naipaul gets sharpened these characters find themselves in an alien strange and diasporic location. They unwillingly get hyphenated identities and if they belong to a particular class, caste and gender they have been treated as subaltern in their land of belonging. This became a stage of doubly marginalized or jeopardy.

In the present scenario immigration is associated with a host of social, economic and political tensions. Migrants are blamed for increasing crime and social disintegration. They provoke fears of reduced wages and increased competition for jobs and social services. The apparently unchecked increase in the numbers of migrants is viewed as a threat to national sovereignty. After 9/11 many fear that the failure to control migration makes countries more vulnerable to terrorism. As a result, the past two decades have witnessed a sharp upsurge in not only migration, but also in xenophobic parties and movements around the world that oppose migration. Faced with these pressures many states seek to sharply curtail migration and turn state borders back into what they once were believed to be – immoveable, impenetrable objects. These social and political forces, taken together, seem to create an unmovable barrier to migration of the people.

Naipaul has presented the same situation in most of his novels where his characters are facing discrimination in alien land because they are not the citizen of that country. They have been marginalized due to caste and location. Today, the writing of Naipaul is quite relevant because his writings have reflected those conditions years back which are happening today.

In the period of globalization, an estimated 232 million people today reside out of the land of their origin, and the numbers are rising rapidly because of blurred boundaries. This massive movement of people across national boundaries is fueled by a host of powerful forces, including the rising demand for both skilled and unskilled labor in developed countries. But for the past few years, they have been facing many racial attacks in all over the world. This is happening because countries are sharpening their national boundaries. The people living away from their country are facing hatred, isolation, discrimination and ethnic problem with the emergence of narrow nationality in many parts of the world including The United State of America. He finds personal reverberation with the worldview of the dispossessed former colonial subject who is busy in the pursuit of establishing their individual identity. Thus, his journey as a prominent diasporic writer writing about subaltern people in terms of caste, class, gender and location ends with a representative author of the suppressed history.

Select Bibliography

Primary Sources:

Fiction:

Naipaul, V. S. *The Mystic Messeur*. London: Andre Deutsch, 1957. Print.

---. *The Suffrage of Elvira*. London: Andre Deutsch, 1958. Print.

---. *Miguel Street*. London: Andre Deutsch, 1959. Print.

---. *A House for Mr. Biswas*. London: Andre Deutsch, 1961. Print.

---. *Mr. Stone and the Knight Companions*. London: Andre Deutsch, 1963. Print.

---. *The Mimic Men*. London: Andre Deutsch, 1967. Print.

---. *A Flag on the Island*. London: Andre Deutsch, 1967. Print.

---. *In a Free State*. London: Andre Deutsch, 1971. Print.

---. *Guerrillas*. London: André Deutsch, 1975. Print.

---. *A Bend in the River*. London: Andre Deutsch, 1979. Print.

---. *The Enigma of Arrival*. London: Viking, 1987. Print.

---. *A Way in the World*. London: Helriman, 1994. Print.

---. *Half a Life*. London: Picador, 2001. Print.

---. *Magic Seeds*. London: Picador, 2004. Print.

Non-Fiction:

Naipaul, V. S. *The Middle Passage*. London: Andre Deutsch, 1962. Print.

---. *An Area of Darkness*. London: Andre Deutsch, 1964. Print.

---. *The Loss of El Dorado*. London: Andre Deutsch, 1969. Print.

---. *The Overcrowded Borraconn.* London: Andre Deutsch, 1972. Print.

---. *India: A Wounded Civilization.* London: Andre Deutsch, 1979. Print.

---. *The Return of Eva Peron with the Killings in Trinidad.* London: Andre Deutsch,

1980. Print.

---. *Among the Believers: An Islamic Journey.* London: Andre Deutsch, 1980. Print.

---. *Findings the Centre: Two Narratives.* London: Andre Deutsch, 1984. Print.

---. *A Turn in the South.* London: Andre Deutsch, 1989. Print.

---. *India: A Million Mutinies Now.* Auckland: Minerva Paperback, 1990. Print.

---. *Beyond: Islamic Excursions among the Converted People.* London: Little Brown,

1998. Print.

Secondary Sources:

Achebe, Chinua. *Things Fall Apart.* New York: Fawcett, 1958. Print.

Alexander, S. M. "Stylish Hard Bodies: Branded Masculinity." *Men's Health*

Magazine: Sociological Perspectives 46.4 (2003): 535-554.

Alexander, V. "Postponed Arrivals: The Afro-Asian Diaspora in M.G. Vassanji's *No*

New Land." Diaspora and Multiculturalism: Common Traditions and New Developments. Ed. M. Fludernik. Amsterdam: Rodopi, 2003. Print.

Allardt, E. "Implications of Ethnic Revival in Modern Industrialized Society: A

Comparative Study of the Linguistic Minorities in Western Europe." *Commenttiones Scientrarum Socialum.* Ed. J. N. Tailor.Helsinki: Scientarum Fennica, 1979. Print.

Anderson, Benedict. *Imagined Community: Reflection on the Origin and Spread of*

Nationalism. London: Verso, 1991. Print.

Angle, Ien. *On Not Speaking Chinese: Living Between Asia and the West.* London:

Routledge, 2001. Print.

Angrésino, Michael. "V. S. Naipaul and the Colonial Image." *Caribbean Quarterly*

2.4 (1975): 2-11. Print

Arnild, Heineman and N. Ramadevi. *The Novels of V. S. Naipaul: Quest for Order and Identity.* New Delhi: Prestige, 1996. Print.

Ashcroft, Bill, Gareth Griffiths and HelenTiffin. *The Empire Writes Back: Theory and Practice Colonial Literatures.* Rutledge: London, 1989. Print.

Ashcroft, Bill. *Key Concept in Postcolonial Studies.* London: Rutledge, 2004. Print.

Ball, John Clement. *Imagining London: Postcolonial Fiction and the Transnational*

Metropolis. Toronto: University of Toronto Press, 2004. Print.

Bama. *Kurukku.* Trnslated by Lakshmi Holmstrom. Chennai: Macmillion, 2000. Print

Beauvior, Simon De. "The Mother." *French Feminism Reader.* Ed. Kelly Oliver. Lanham: Rowaman, 2000. Print.

Beck, Ulrich, and Natan Sznaider. "Unpacking Cosmopolitanism for the Social

Sciences: A Research Agenda." *The British Journal of Sociology* 57.1 (2006): 1-23. Print.

Bell, Daniel. "Ethnicity & Social Change". *Ethnicity: Theory and Experience*. Eds.

N. Glazer & D. P. Moynihan. Cambridge: Harvard University Press, 1975. 141-174.

Bhabha, Homi. *Nation and Narration*. London: Routledge, 1990. Print.

---. *Location of Culture*. London: Rutledge, 1994. Print.

---. "Dissemination: Time, Narrative and the Margins of the Modern Nation." *Nation*

and Narration. Ed. Homi Bhabha. London: Routledge, 1990. Print.

Bhal, Vinay. "Relevance or Irrelevance of Subaltern Studies." *Reading Subaltern*

Studies. Ed. S. P. Trivedi. Orient: Longman, 2002. Print.

Bhargara, Rajul. *Indian Writing In English: The Last Decade*. New Delhi: Rawat Publications, 2002. Print.

Bharucha, Nilufer. *Rohinton Mistry: Ethnic Enclosures and Transcultural Spaces*.

Jaipur: Rawat Publication, 2003.Print.

Boehmer, Elleke. *Colonial and Postcolonial Literature: Migrant Metaphors*. New

York: Oxford University Press, 1995. Print.

Borradori, G. *Philosophy in a Time of Terror: Dialogues with Jiirgen Habermas and Jacques Derrida*. Chicago: University of Chicago Press, 2003. Print.

Boxill, Anthony. *V. S. Naipaul's Fiction: In Quest of the Enemy*. New Brunswick: York Press, 1983. Print.

---. *The Little Bastard World of V. S. Naipaul's The Mimic Men* and *A Flag on the Island. Pdf.* Web. 04 Sep. 2012. 12-19.

Bryden, Roland. Interview with V.S. Naipaul. The Literature. Vol. 89. 25 January,

2015.

Burnett, Edward Tylor. *Primitive Culture.* New York: Holt, 1877. Print.

Butler, Judith. *Gender Trouble: Feminism and the Subversion of Identity.* London: Routledge, 1990. Print.

Chakrabarty, Dipesh. "Invitation to a Dialogue." *Subaltern Studies.* Ed. Ranajit Guha.

Delhi: OUP, 1985. Print.

Chakravarti, Uma. *Gendering Caste: Through a Feminist Lens.* Calcutta: Street, 2006.

Print.

Chandra. N. D. R. *Contemporary Indian Writing in English.* New Delhi: Sarup and Sons Publication, 2008. Print.

Clarkson, J. "Contesting Masculinity's Makeover: Queer Eye, Consumer Masculinity,

and Straight Acting Gays." *Journal of Communication Inquiry* 29.3 (2005): 235-255.

Cooke, John. "A Vision of the Land: V. S. Naipaul's Later Novels." *Journal of*

Caribbean Studies 24.1(1980): 140-61 Print.

Connell, R. W. "An Iron Man: The Body and Some Contradictions of Hegemonic

Masculinity." *Sport, Men and the Gender Order: Critical Feminist Perspectives.* Eds. M. A. Meissner and D. F. Sabo. Champaign: Human Kinetics, 1990. 83-95.

Cudjoe, Selwvan R. *V.S. Naipaul a Materialist Reading.* Amherst: University of

Massachusetts Press, 1988. Print.

Das, B. K. *Twentieth Century Literacy Criticisms.* Delhi: Atlantic, 2005. Print.

David, Guralnic, ed. *Webster's New World College Dictionary,* 3rd ed. 1997. Print.

De Kock, Leon. "Interview with Gayatri Chakravorty Spivak: New Nation Writers Conference in South Africa." *Ariel: A Review of International English Literature*. 1992. Print.

Delanty, Gerard. "The Cosmopolitan Imagination: Critical Cosmopolitanism and Social Theory." *The British Journal of Sociology* 57.1 (2006): 25-47. Print.

Derrick, A. C. "Naipaul's Technique as a Novelist." *The Journal of Commonwealth Literature* 12.3 (1969): 32-33. Print.

Dhawan, R. K. *Writers of Indian Diaspora*. New Delhi: Prestige Books, 2001. Print.

Dirks, N. B., ed. *Colonialism and Culture*. Ann Arbor: University of Michigan Press, 1975. Print.

Eagleton, Marry and David Pierce. *Attitude to Class in the English Novel*. London: Thomas and Hudson, 1979. Print.

Fanon, Frantz. *Black Skin, White Masks*. New York: Grove Press, 1967. Print.

Foucault, Michel. *The Archaeology of Knowledge*. New York: Pantheon, 1972. Print.

French, Patrick. *The World Is What It Is: The Authorized Biography of V. S. Naipaul*. New York: Alfred Knopf, 2008. Print.

Fromm, Erich. *Escape from Freedom*. New York: Rinehart, 1941. Print.

Gandhi, Leela. *Postcolonial Theory: A Critical Introduction*. New Delhi: Oxford University Press, 1998. Print.

Garebian, Keith. "V. S. Naipaul's Negative Sense of Place." *The Journal of Commonwealth Literature* 25.2 (1975): 30-32.

Geetha, V. *Gender: Theorizing Feminism.* New Delhi: Stree, 2001. Print.

Genetsch, M. *The Texture of Identity: The Fiction of M. G. Vassanji, Neil Bissoondath and Rohinton Mistry.* Toronto: TSAR Publications, 2007. Print.

Greenhalgh, Susan. *Madoc-Jones.* London: OUP, 1966. Print.

Grosu, Lucia-Mihaela. *Mapping the Road to Identity in V. S. Naipaul's Magic.* London: Oxford University Press, 2013. Print.

Guha, Ranajit. "On Aspects of the Historiography of Colonial India." *Mapping Subaltern Studies and the Postcolonial.* Ed. Vinayak Charturvedi. London: Verso, 2000. Print.

---. ed. *Subaltern Studies: Writings on South Asian History and Society* (7 Volumes). Delhi: OUP, 1982. Print.

--- . ed. *Subaltern Studies II:* The Prose of Counter Insurgency.Delhi: OUP, 1982. Print.

--- . *Elementary Aspects of Peasant Insurgency in Colonial India.* Delhi: OUP, 1983. Print.

Gupta, Suman. *V.S. Naipaul.* United Kingdom: Northcote House Pub, 1999. Print.

Gussow, Mel. "The Enigma of V. S. Naipaul's Search for Himself in Writing." *New York Times.* 25 April, 1987. Print.

---. "Travel Plus Writing Plus Reflection Equals V.S. Naipaul." T*he New York Times.* http://query. mytimes. com/gst/fullpage.html? January 30, 1991.

--- . *Writer Without Roots.* New York: Vintage, 1976.

Hadden, A. C. *The Wandering of Peoples.* Cambridge: Cambridge University Press, 1912. Print.

Hall, Stuart. "Cultural Identity and Diaspora." *Theorizing Diaspora: A Reader.* Ed.

Jana Evan Braziel and Anita Mannur. London: Blackwell Publishing Ltd, 2003.

Halloran, Thomas F. "Politics and Identity in V. S. Naipaul's Third World." *Atenea*

27.1 (2007): 121-34. Print.

Hamner, Robert D. *Critical Perspectives on V. S. Naipaul.* London: Heinemann Educational Books, 1979. Print.

Hanke, R. "Hegemonic Masculinity in Something." *Critical Studies in Mass*

Communication 7.3 (1990): 231-248. Print.

Hawthorn, Jeremy. *A Glossary of Contemporary Theory,* London: Arnold, 2000.

Print.

Herek, G. M. "On Heterosexual Masculinity: Some Psychical Consequences of the

Social Construction of Gender and Sexuality." *Changing Men: New Direction in Research on Men and Masculinity.* Ed. M. S. Kimmel.Newbury Park: Sage, 1987. Print.

Hulme, Peter. *The Cambridge Companion to Travel Writing.* London: University of

Essex, 2002.Print.

Jain, Jasbir. "Problems of Postcolonial Literatures." *Problems of Postcolonial Literatures and Other Essays.* Ed. Jain Jasbir. Jaipur: Print well, 1991. 1-15.

---. *Writers of Indian Diaspora: Theory and Practice.* Jaipur: Rawat Publication, 1998. Print.

Jayaram, N. The *Indian Diaspora: Dynamics of Migration.* New Delhi: Sage

Publications, 2004. Print.

Kakar, Sudhir. *The Inner World.* New Delhi: Oxford University Press, 1992. Print.

Karma, Shashi. *The Novels of V.S. Naipaul: A Study in Theme and Form.* New Delhi:

Prestige, 1990. Print.

Kasdan, Lenard. "Introduction." *Migration and Anthropology Proceeding of the 1970 Annual Spring Meeting of the American, Ethnological Society.* Eds. F. Spencer and L. Kasdan. London: University of Washington Press, 1970. 1-6 Print.

Khair, Tabish. *Babu Fiction: Alienation in Contemporary Indian English Novels.* New Delhi: Oxford University Press, 2005.

Khan, Fawzia Afzal. *Cultural Imperialism and Indo-English Fiction.* New York:

OUP, 1995. Print.

Khan, Md. Akhtar. *V.S. Naipaul: A Critical Study.* New Delhi: Creative Books, 1998. Print.

King, Bruce. *V. S. Naipaul.* London: Macmillan, 1993. Print.

--- . *Modern Novelist: V. S. Naipaul.* London: Macmillan Press, 1989. Print.

--- . "Introduction." *West Indian Literature.* London: Macmillan, 1979. Print.

Kipling, Rudyard. *Best of Attack and National Vangard.* London: The National Alliance, 2005. Print.

Lamming, George. *The Pleasures of Exile.* London: Joseph, 1960. Print.

Lin, C. L. and J. T. Yeh. "Comparing Society's Awareness of Women: Media-

Portrayed Idealized Images and Physical Attractiveness." *Journal of Business Ethics* 90.1 (2009):

61–79. Print.

Loomba, Ania and Suvir Kaul, eds. *On India: Writing History, Culture, Post-*

Coloniality. Special Issue of Oxford Literary Review 16.2 (1994): 23-34. Print.

Lowenthal, David. *West Indian Societies.* New York: University Press, 1972. Print.

Ludden, David, ed. *Reading Subaltern Studies.* Delhi: Permanent Black, 2001. Print.

Melman, Billie. "The Middle East/Arabia: The Cradle of Islam." *The Cambridge*

Companion to Travel Writing. Eds. Peter Hulme and Tim Youngs. Cambridge: Cambridge University Press, 2002. Print.

Memmi, Albert. *The Colonizer and the Colonized.* Boston: Beacon Press, 1967. Print.

Menchu, Rigoberta. *I, Rigoberta Menchu: An Indian Women in Guatemala.* Trans. by

Ann Wright. London: Verso, 1994. Print.

Mishra, Vijay. "New Lamps for Old: Diasporas Migrancy Border." *Commonwealth*

Writing: A Study in Expatriate Experience. Eds. R. K. Dhawan and L.S.R. Krishna Sastry. New Delhi: Prestige Books, 1994. Print.

Mishra, Vijay and Bob Hodge. "What Is Post (-) Colonialism?" *Colonial Discourse*

And Postcolonial Theory: A Reader. Eds. Patrick Williams and Laura Chrisman. New York: Columbia University Press, 1994. 276-290.

Mishra, Sudesh. "From Sugar to Masala: Writing by the Indian Diaspora." *A Rupkatha.* Ed. Arvind Krishna Mehrotra, Kolkata: Permanent Black, 2003.

Mittapalli, Rajeshwar and Micheal Hensen, eds. *V.S. Naipaul: Fiction and Travel Writing*. New Delhi: Atlantic, 2002. Print.

Mohan, Champa Rao. *Postcolonial Situation in the Novels of V. S. Naipaul*. New

Delhi: Atlantic Publisher and Distributers, 2004. Print.

Morton, Stephen. *Gayatri Chakrovorty Spivak*. Oxon: Routledge, 2003. Print.

Moslund, Sten Pultz. *Migration Literature and Hybridity: The Different Speeds of*

Transcultural Change. Basingstoke: Palgrave Macmillan, 2010. Print.

Mukherjee, Arun Prabha. *Postcolonialism: My Living*. Toronto: TSAR, 1998. Print.

Mustapha, Nasser. "The Influence of Indian Islam on Fundamentalist Trends in Trinidad and Tabogo." *The Indian Diaspora: Dynamics of Migration*. Ed. N. Jayaram. New Delhi: Sage Publication, 2004. Print.

Mustafa, Fawzia. *V.S. Naipaul*. New York: Cambridge University Press, 1995. Print.

Naipaul, V. S. "Conrad's Darkness." *Critical Perspectives of V. S. Naipaul*. Ed. Robert D. Hammer. London: Heinimann, 1997. Print.

Naipaul, V.S. "Prologue to an Autobiography." *Literary Occasions: Essays*. Ed. Pankaj Mishra. New Delhi: Picadore, 2003. Print.

---. "Floating up to a Point." Interview with *Guardian*. 30 April, 1984. Print.

Naipaul,V. S. "Writer Without Roots." *The New York Times Magazines*. Dec 26,

1976. 19-22. Print.

Nandan, Satendra. "The Diasporic Consciousness: From Biswas to Biswasghat."

Interrogation Postcolonialism. Eds. Meenakshi Mukherjee and Harish Trivedi. Shimla: Indian Institute of Advanced Study, 1996. Print.

Nandy, Ashis. "Preface." *The Intimate Enemy: Loss and Recovery of Self under Colonialism.* Ed. R. K. Dhawan. New Delhi: Oxford University Press, 1983. Print.

Nayar, Pramod K. *Postcolonial Literature: An Introduction.* New Delhi: Pearson,

2008. Print.

Nehru, Pt. J. L. *The Discovery of India.* Calcutta: The Signet Press, 1946. Print.

Niranjana, Tejaswini. *Mobilizing India: Women, Music and Migration Between India*

and Trinidad. North Carolina: Duke University Press, 2006. Print.

Niven, Alastari. "V. S. Naipaul Talks to Alastair Niven." *Wasafiri* 10.21 (1995): 5-6.

Print.

Nixon, Rob. *Review: V. S. Naipaul and Postcolonial Mandarin.* (1991): 100-113.

<http://www.jstor.org> Thu Jan 4 2007.

Ormerod, David. "In a Derelict Land." *Critical Perspective on V. S. Naipaul.* Ed. R.D. Hammer. Washington D. C.: Three Continents Press, 1977. Print.

Pandey, Dr. Jaishankar. *Prachin Bhartiya Samaj Ewan Sanskriti.* Delhi: Prachya

Bharti, 1987. Print.

Panwar, Purabi. *V. S. Naipaul: An Anthology of Recent Criticism.* Delhi: Pencraft International, 2003. Print.

Paranjape, Makarand. "Triple Ambivalence: Australia, Canada, and South Asia in the Diasporic Imagination." *Journal of the Department of English* 32.2. Eds. Sanjukta Dasgupta and Jharna Sanyal, Kolkata: Calcutta University,

2005-2006.

---. "Coping with Post Colonialism." *Interrogating Post–Colonialism: Theory, Text and Context*. Eds. Sanjukta Dasgupta and Jharna Sanyal. Rutledge: London, 1990. Print.

Park, Robert E., ed. "Human Migration and the Marginal Man" *Race and Culture*. Glencoe: The Free Press, 1950. Print.

Peter, Hulme. "Travelling to Write (1940-2000)." *The Cambridge Companion to*

Travel Writing. Eds. Peter Hulme and Tim Youngs. Cambridge: Cambridge University Press, 2002. Print.

Pronger, B. *The Arena of Masculinity: Sports, Homosexuality, and the Meaning of*

Sex. New York: St. Martin's Press. 1990. Print.

Rai, Sudha. *V. S. Naipaul: A Study in Expatriate Sensibility*. New Delhi: Atlantic,

2002. Print.

Rao, Mdhusudana. *Contrary Awareness: A Critical Study of V. S. Naipaul's Novels.*

Gunter: Sarathe, 1982. Print.

Renan, Ernest. "What is a Nation?" *Nation and Narration*. Ed.Homi K. Bhabha.

London: Rutledge, 1990. Print.

Riggs, Fred. W. *Ethnicity: Intercocta Glossary, Concepts and Terms Used in*

Ethnicity Research 4. Paris: Hawai SocialScience Council, UNESCO, 1985. Print.

Rubin, G. "Thinking Sex: Notes for a radical theory of the politics of sexuality."

Pleasure and danger: Exploring Female Sexuality. Ed. C. Vance.Boston: Routledge, 1985. 267-319. Print.

Rushdie, Salman. *Imaginary Homelands: Essays and Criticism 1981 – 1991*. London: Granta Bo University,

1996. Print.

Rushdie, Salman. *Midnight's Children.* New York: Vintage, 1981. Print.

--- . "Cry My Beloved Country." *Hindu Magazine* 18 June, 2000. Print.

Safran, William. "Diaspora in Modern Societies: Myths of Homeland and Return." *Diaspora: A Journal of Transnational Studies* 1.1 (1991): 12-18.

Sahoo, Ajay Kumar. *Transnational-Indian Diaspora.* New Delhi: Abhijeet Publication, 2006. Print.

Said, Edward. "Two Visions in Heart of Darkness." *Culture and Imperialism (*1993): 22-31. *Pdf.* Web. 04 Sep. 2012.

--- . *Culture and Imperialism.* London: Vintage, 1994. Print.

Sarangi, Jaideep. "Bond Without Bondage: Bharati Mukherjee and Jumpa Lahiri." *Studies in Women Writers in English.* Eds. Mohit K. Ray and Rama Kandu. New Delhi: Atlantic Publishers, 2005. 139-149.

Sarkar, Sumit, ed. "The Decline of the Subaltern." *Writing Social History.* Delhi: OUP, 1997. Print.

Sen, Asok. "Subaltern Studies: Capital, Class and Community." *Subaltern Studies V: Writing on South Asian History and Society.* Ed. Ranajit Guha. Delhi: Oxford UP, 1987. 203-35. Print.

Sharma, Ursula. *Caste.* Kolkata: Viva, 2005. Print.

Sherlock, Phillp. *West Indian Nations: A New History.* New York: St. Martinis Press, 1973. Print.

Shuval, Judith. "Diaspora Migration: Definitional Ambiguities and a Theoretical Paradigm." *International Migration* 38.5 (2000): 41-56. Print.

Singh, Manjit Inder. *V. S. Naipaul.* New Delhi: Rawat Publication, 1998. Print.

Spivak, Gayatri Chakravorti. *In Other Worlds: Essays in Cultural Politics.* New York: Routledge, 1987. Print.

Statesville, J. R. "Sexually Polarized Products and Advertising Strategy." *Journal of*

Retailing 47.2 (1971): 3-13. Print.

Szerszynski, Bronislaw and John Urry. "Cultures of Cosmopolitanism." *The*

Sociological Review 50.4 (2002): 461-81. Print.

Teltscher, Kate. "India/Calcutta: City of Palaces and Dreadful Night." *The Cambridge Companion to Travel Writing.* Eds. Peter Hulme and Tim Youngs. Cambridge: Cambridge University Press, 2002. Print.

Tharoor, Shashi. *A Glossary of Indianess: Sunday Times of India*, Lucknow, May 7,

2007. Print.

Theroux, Paul. *V. S. Naipaul: A Introduction to His Work.* London: Andre Deutsch, 1972. Print.

Thieme, John. "Calypso Allusions in Naipaul's *Miguel Street.*" *Kunapipi* 3.2 (1981):

18-33. Print.

Thiong, Wo, Ngugi. "The Language of African Literature." (2011): 435-445. *Pdf.*

Web. 04 Sep. 2012.

Thompson, C. J. "Marketplace Mythology and Discourses of Power." *Journal of*

Consumer Research 31.1 (2004): 162-180. Print.

Thorpe, Michael. *Writersand Their Work: V.S. Naipaul.* Edinburgh: Longman Group,

1976. Print.

Trujillo, N. "Hegemonic Masculinity on the Mound: Media Representations of Nolan

Ryan and American Sports Culture." *Critical Studies in Mass Communication* 8.3 (1991): 290-308. Print.

Vassanji, M. G. *The Gunny Sack*. London: Heinemann, 1989. Print.

---. The *In-Between World of Vikram Lall*. New York: Knopf, 2004. Print.

--- . *No New Land*. New York:Mclelland and Sterwart, 1991. Print.

Report Government of India. New Delhi: Publication Division-Ministry of

Information and Broadcasting, 1996: 744-50. Print.

Walder, Dennis. *Post-colonial Literature in English: History, Language and Theory*. Oxford: Blackwell, 2005. Print.

Weiss, Timthy F. *On the Margin: The Art of Exile in V.S. Naipaul*. Amherst:

Massachusetts Press, 1992. Print.

White, Landeg. *V. S. Naipaul: A Critical Introduction*. London: The Macmillan Press, 1975.

William, Eric. *From Columbus to Castro: The History of the Caribbean: 1492-1969*.New York: Harper & Row, 1970. Print.

Wolfrey, Juluian. *Key Concepts in Literary Theory*. London: Oxford Publication,

1984. Print.

Wörsching, M. "Race to the Top: Masculinity, Sport, and Nature."*Men and*

Masculinity 10.2 (2007): 197-221. Print.

Young, Robert. *Post- Colonialism: A Very Short Introduction*. New York: Oxford

University Press, 2003. Print.

Nobel Prize for Literature 2001 - Press Release. *Nobelprize.org*. Nobel Media AB 2014. http://www.nobelprize.org/nobel_prizes/literature/laureates/2001/press.html

https://books.google.co.in/books

http://www.encyclopedia.com/topic/V. S. Naipaul.aspx

http://en.wikipedia.org/wiki/V. S. Naipaul

http://www.jstor.org/stable/

www.ingramcontent.com/pod-product-compliance
Ingram Content Group UK Ltd.
Pitfield, Milton Keynes, MK11 3LW, UK
UKHW040005200726
13854UKWH00001B/44